W9-CAS-692

The House That Cleans Itself

Mindy Starns Clark

HARVEST HOUSE PUBLISHERS
EUGENE, OREGON

McMasters United Methodis'
Church Library

All Scripture quotations are taken from the HOLY BIBLE, NEW INTERNATIONAL VERSION®. NIV®. Copyright © 1973, 1978, 1984 by the International Bible Society. Used by permission of Zondervan. All rights reserved.

To protect the privacy of individuals who completed my housekeeping surveys and/or shared their stories, names have been changed throughout this book.

Some graphics inside this book were created by Linda Moye, with additional graphics by Amy Starns and Steve Kuhn. Used by permission.

Cover illustration © Michael Lotenero / Photodisc Green / Getty Images

Cover by The Dugan Design Group, Bloomington, Minnesota

THE HOUSE THAT CLEANS ITSELF
Copyright © 2007 by Mindy Starns Clark
Published by Harvest House Publishers
Eugene, Oregon 97402
www.harvesthousepublishers.com

Clark, Mindy Starns.
The house that cleans itself / Mindy Starns Clark.
p. cm.
ISBN 13: 978-0-7369-1880-0 (pbk.)

1. House cleaning. 2. Christian life. I. Title
TX324.C576 2007
648'.5—dc22

2007004335

All rights reserved. No part of this publication may be reproduced, stored in a retrieval system, or transmitted in any form or by any means—electronic, mechanical, digital, photocopy, recording, or any other—except for brief quotations in printed reviews, without the prior permission of the publisher.

Printed in the United States of America

09 10 11 12 13 14 / VP-SK / 10

Dedicated with much love to my dear friend
Kay Justus.
Thanks for putting up with me as a roommate all those years ago
when housekeeping was not exactly my forte,
the vacuum cleaner got more use as a coat rack,
and the oven was for hiding dirty dishes.

That was then, this is now...

Acknowledgments

To perfect the HTCI System and write this book, I utilized the help of several wonderful internet groups. Offering anonymity in exchange for information, I was able to survey hundreds of people with some basic housekeeping questions as well as dig deeper with follow-up interviews to those who chose to respond in detail. I am deeply indebted to the people who were willing to share their deepest messy-house secrets, fears, and feelings. Because many graciously revealed unflattering facts, I've changed most of the names used throughout this book to protect their privacy.

To all of my anonymous internet helpers: You know who you are, and my hope is that upon reading this book you're glad you chose to be so transparent to help all who struggle in the area of housekeeping. I am indebted to each of you. Thank you!

I am also so very thankful to:

Linda Moye, for the adorable sketches created for this book. You have a wonderful talent and a godly spirit, and it's a pleasure to work with you.

Amy Starns, for additional contributions to the artwork. Your talents never cease to amaze me.

"Dr. Gadget," AKA Dave Dettman, for showing me the latest and greatest in household cleaning devices.

Harvest House Publishers, for being so great, as always, and to Barbara Gordon, who sweetly helped craft this book into an organized whole.

Shari Weber, for your editorial advice, input, and friendship, and to Jackie Starns, for expert proofreading.

To the lovely ladies of my LIFL group, and to Elisa Marshall, who helped me look back in order to move forward. You are such a blessing in my life!

The Clarks, Scannells, Kings, and Sullivans, whose housekeeping skills I have long admired.

The members of Chi Libris and ACFW, for your companionship, support, and incredible wisdom.

My daughters, Emily and Lauren, for all you do to make this happen.

And last but not least, my husband, John, for all your help in organizing my thoughts on this topic and for loving me so completely. You are my helpmate, my soul mate, and my best friend.

Contents

A Better Way 7
A Creative Approach 11

Part 1: Get Ready...

Step 1: Draw a Floor Plan and Determine Flow Pattern ... 21
Step 2: Decide on Your Home Base Zone 27
Step 3: Involve the Household and Hang the Signs 33
Step 4: Put God at the Center 41
Step 5: Gather Tools and Document Evidence 47
Step 6: Evaluate Evidence 53
Step 7: Consider the Clutter 59
Step 8: Comprehend You, Your Brain, and the Mess 65
Step 9: Estimate, Commit, Plan 77
Step 10: Create a Devotional Area 85

Part 2: Get Set...

Introducing the CONVERT System 93
11. **C** lear Out the Clutter 97
12. **O** pen Up and Clean 107
13. **N** eaten, Organize, and Solve Problem Spots 111
14. **V** erify Rabbit Trails and Set Up Stations 123
15. **E** xamine Sight Zones 141
16. **R** ecord Future Improvements Needed 147
17. **T** ake Steps Now for Ongoing Maintenance 151
18. The Checklist 161

Part 3: Go!

19. Work Your Way Through the House 167
20. How to Clean a House That Cleans Itself 191
21. Doing the Paper Two-Step 211

Part 4: From Me to You

22. My Journey to Clean 225
23. A Final Word 233

A Better Way

By wisdom a house is built, and through understanding it is established; through knowledge its rooms are filled with rare and beautiful treasures.

PROVERBS 24:3-4

Mary Poppins has always been my hero. I can remember sitting in a darkened movie theater as a child, watching the screen, mesmerized by the most astounding movie scene I had ever seen. As I watched, my heart pounded, my soul soared, and I yearned for Mary Poppins to leap out from the screen, take my hand, and bring me along on her miraculous adventure. What in the movie captivated me so?

Was it the nanny gently parachuting to the ground with only the help of an umbrella? Was it the sight of her jumping into a chalk drawing on a sidewalk and landing in an alternate cartoon universe? No. It was the scene where she simply snaps her fingers and a messy bedroom begins to get clean. *By itself!*

I can still remember the sight of drawers flying open, clothes folding and inserting themselves into dressers, toys leaping into the toy box. With a little girl's awe, I was savvy enough to know that the scene wasn't real—but deep in my heart I wished it could be. Surely somewhere, somehow, there really was a house that could clean itself.

In retrospect, it's not surprising that was the scene from *Mary*

Poppins that most resonated with me. I already had two loving parents so I didn't need a nanny dropping in out of the sky, and my life was already fun so I didn't really yearn to leap into a sidewalk and ride a cartoon merry-go-round. But even as a young child I was already hopeless at cleaning. My bedroom was even messier than the one in the movie. I would have given anything to have Mary Poppins dispatch the disaster there—and when she finished, I'd have her go room by room through the entire house, helping my mom out too.

Now these many years later, I'd still love to get a visit from Mary Poppins. The truth is, I don't like cleaning or organizing. Consequently I have struggled for most of my life with messiness: ignoring it, trying to conquer it, surrendering to it, fighting it, feeling ashamed by it, giving up on it, trying again to conquer it. The struggle has drained my energy, my self-esteem, and my resources. It has strained relationships, cost me valuable time and money, and prevented me from doing a number of things I would otherwise have been able to do.

As a novelist, I usualy make the homes of my heroines spotlessly clean. But in reality, for many years my home was anything but. So why am I, of all people, qualified to write a book called *The House That Cleans Itself?* Because after a lifetime of failure at the conventional methods of cleaning and organizing, I have finally come to understand that for those of us who struggle in this area, *there is a better way.* Through sheer frustration with my own mess, I turned to research and prayer, trial and error, testing and questioning, until I figured out how to get my house clean and keep it that way most of the time—despite my shortcomings. You might even say that because I wasn't any good at cleaning my house, I created a way for my house to clean itself.

That's not to say that I never have to lift a finger to keep my home clean. But if you were to compare the amount of time I used to spend cleaning to the amount of time I spend cleaning now, you would understand that I have drastically cut that time—not by changing myself but by *changing my house.* More importantly, if you could see how messy my home used to be despite my best efforts, and how clean it is now, with far less work, you would agree that something very significant changed around here.

I still haven't found a way to make clothes float into the air and fold themselves or have toys jump into a toy box. What I have found is a way to streamline the housecleaning process to a minimum of time by making adjustments, both large and small, to my surroundings. In this book I will show you how to apply my concepts to your mess so that you too can conquer your housekeeping woes once and for all. Follow the plan laid out in this book and you too will have a house that cleans itself.

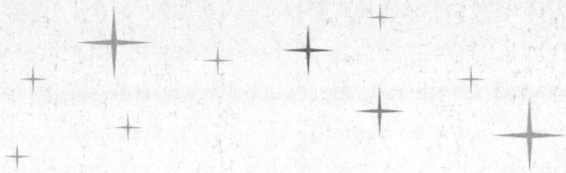

Introduction

A Creative Approach

So what is this book exactly? *The House That Cleans Itself* is a how-to guide that reveals, step-by-step, a system that will:

- take a house that *tends to be messy* and turn it into a house that *tends to be neat*
- take a cleaning routine that takes up *far too much time* and turn it into a cleaning routine that is *shockingly fast*
- take a family that struggles with *mess-inducing behaviors* and turn it into a family with *naturally tidy behaviors,* often without family members even realizing it
- take a life where *the minutes are eaten away* by ordinary household tasks and turn it into a life with *time to spare* for things that really count
- take a person who *feels like a failure* in caring for his or her home and change that person into someone who is unburdened, unashamed, and *successful* in caring for the home

When done correctly, The House That Cleans Itself System will guide you and your family through a process that will make your home easier to keep clean, easier to manage, and easier to enjoy.

How Does the System Work?

The House That Cleans Itself (HTCI) System begins by leading you step-by-step through a home-evaluation process. By taking a fresh look at familiar spaces, you will be able to define the various behaviors and habits that tend to create clutter, mess, and dirt throughout your home. Conventional housekeeping experts might say that once you know what the problem behaviors and habits are, you can change them. But I contend that if you *could* change those behaviors you *would* have done so by now. In fact, you've probably tried and tried in the past and ended up disappointed and frustrated with yourself and/or your family members.

By adapting the environment to compensate for and/or eliminate the behavior, your house will stay clean longer and with less effort than you ever imagined.

The HTCI System, however, shows you how to *change your house,* often in creative and clever ways, so that behaviors are no longer an issue. By adapting the *environment* to compensate for and/or eliminate the *behavior,* your house will stay clean longer and with less effort than you ever imagined.

Finally, my system shows you how to maintain lasting change—again, not by forcing you to develop new habits and behaviors, but by anticipating and circumventing your natural inclinations toward mess from now on.

If you follow the system from beginning to end, faithfully doing each step, when you are finished your house will stay cleaner day by day and your cleaning routine will be faster and more efficient than ever before. Best of all, these things will happen in a way that at times feels so effortless you'll think your house really is cleaning itself!

Still not quite clear on how it works? Let me give you some tangible examples.

In a House That's a Struggle to Clean	*In a House That Cleans Itself*
You bring in the day's mail, flip through it for anything good or interesting, and toss the rest on the table until you have time to fool with it	You bring in the day's mail, flip through it for anything good or interesting, and drop the rest into the Standing Paper Sorter so it's on its way to being dealt with.
When you find clothes you no longer want, you put them aside to eventually give to charity. The items sit as a pile of clutter in your room or work their way back into your closet.	When you find clothes you no longer want, you put them into your Upstairs Charity Bucket to give to charity. When you have time, all you do is lift out the plastic liner, tie it off, toss it into your car, and go. Bonus: Because you have somewhere to put such items, you've added others, preventing further clutter and giving you a bigger donation.
You hang on to an entire shelf filled with cookbooks even though you only use a few recipes from each.	You tear out the pages that have recipes you like, put those in a recipe box or self-stick photo album, and recycle the rest of the books, clearing out half the shelf.
You nag your kids endlessly to stop dumping their backpacks beside the front door.	You provide an attractive cabinet or trunk or container that's big enough to hold your kids' backpacks and place it beside the front door.

As you can see, this system combines logic with creativity to solve mess-inducing challenges all over your house.

The Road Ahead

As you may have guessed by now, working your way through the steps of the HTCI System is going to require some time and effort. *But it's worth it because it works!!*

Please understand that the goal is not a *perfect* house. Ironically, perfectionism actually makes your home worse, not better. No, our goal is a *clean-enough* house, one where kids can make messes but those messes get cleaned up when they're done; where dad can dirty every pot in the house whipping up a gourmet dessert, but those pots are washed and put away in a reasonable amount of time; where mom can sit on the couch and close her eyes once in a while, not because she's overwhelmed by the mess but because she's relaxed by the clean. The goal is a living, breathing, working home that allows for life but recovers quickly and easily from the messes that life inevitably brings. In a HTCI, a house is *clean* when:

- the rooms have the pleasing appearance of neatness
- all surfaces are adequately clean
- the closets and drawers are well organized so they serve as fully functioning tools for daily living
- the systems for accomplishing household tasks are working smoothly for every member of the family
- the odds and ends of life are easily processed and not allowed to form clutter

If that definition of clean resonates with you, keep reading! By tossing out perfectionist standards that are impossible to achieve, your home will actually become *clean enough* much more consistently than ever before.

Self Assessment

To begin to get a handle on the cleaning problems in your home, consider whether any of the following statements are true for you as they were for most of the respondents of my housekeeping survey.

"Keeping the house neat and/or clean is a challenge for me because I am not naturally gifted at housekeeping."

Cleaning is a necessity for all of us, sure, but for some fortunate people it's also a talent—a natural, instinctive ability and inclination. Those of us who are more "housekeeping challenged" might often say, "I've got to do a better job of keeping my house clean" or "I really need to get my act together in this area"—as if it's purely a matter of will and discipline. Will and discipline are important in many ways, but I contend that *at its very core, success or failure as a housekeeper is most strongly linked with natural, innate ability.* If you have spent years thinking your biggest problem was that you lacked character or self-discipline, think again. Your biggest problem may be that your brain is simply not hard-wired toward cleaning.

Sure you can make your house spotless when you absolutely have to. But if keeping your home clean on a consistent basis is a struggle, you're probably just not gifted in this area. The great news is that the HTCI System will show you how to compensate for a lack of natural ability so your house will stay clean anyway.

1. *"Keeping the house neat and/or clean is a challenge for me because I was never really taught how to clean."*

I'm not implying that no one ever showed you how to work a mop or scrub a toilet. You may have plenty of "head knowledge" about cleaning skills. You may have even read books about it or taken classes or sought advice from experts. But if the cleanliness and/or organization of your home is a challenge despite that knowledge, there is a disconnect between what you *know* and what you *do.* Chances are that disconnect is rooted in the fact that what you *learned* was vastly different from what you *lived.* Instruction is not sufficient without example, and example is not sufficient without instruction. If you lacked either instruction *or* example while growing up, you more than likely don't possess a full knowledge of the subject, even if you've invested a lot of effort in figuring it out since.

When Julie's children were small, she spent a lot of time patiently teaching them about the different techniques of cleaning. She didn't consistently model those techniques in their home, which was usually a mess. For example, Julie taught her daughter how to cook a meal, but she never modeled good meal planning—in fact, she rarely thought about what she was going to serve for dinner until the kids were cranky, her husband was starving, and the sun had long set. She was giving them instruction without example.

Beth, on the other hand, was too busy cleaning to take the time to teach her children how to clean at all. She did, however, model cleaning behavior almost all day, every day, by keeping a beautiful home. Beth did expect her children to do their share, but she would bellow out broad commands like "Go clean your room!" without ever taking the time to show her children how to approach an entire room and put it in order. In the end, frustrated with their mediocre efforts, she would do it herself. She was providing example without instruction.

2. *"Keeping the house neat and/or clean is a challenge for me because the entire subject of cleaning carries a lot of emotional baggage."*

Is housekeeping a loaded issue for you? It sure is for Donna. Raised by a critical mother, Donna gave up trying years ago. She bristles whenever anyone suggests that she get her act together and clean up her house. *Why should I?* she wonders. *What's the point? I'll never measure up anyway.*

Frank grew up in a very poor family where there was hardly ever enough of anything. Now an adult with a well-paying job and a good home, he can't bear to clear out the stuff that fills his home from one end to the other. It's almost as if he has to keep everything out where he can see it to reassure himself that he'll never have to go without again.

There are a number of emotional and/or physical reasons we hang on to clutter, resist change, and choose to ignore the disasters around us. For example, if your housekeeping problems are severe, you may need to be evaluated by your doctor for Attention Defecit Disorder (ADD) or Obsessive compulsive Disorder (OCD). Often, however, simply recognizing the origins of your housekeeping baggage may be all you need to get started on the path to change. As you think about the emotions you have that relate to cleaning, allow God to give you insights and healing as you delve into your feelings. With help, you can work through the emotional impediments to a clean house if you're willing to be honest and commit to the process of growth and change.

The startling truth (well, startling to those of us who struggle with housekeeping) is that *cleaning really shouldn't have any emotional component at all.* It's not an emotional subject. It's just a necessary set of tasks. If the thought of cleaning house evokes any sort of emotion at all other than something between vague weariness and mild pleasure—for example, if you *despise* it or you *crave* it—then it's time to unpack that baggage and see what's in there. It's weighing you down and making housekeeping, which is just a necessary part of life, much more difficult than it needs to be.

The Bottom Line

Most housekeeping books tell you to change your behavior, but I say, if you lack talent and/or know-how, or are hindered by emotional issues, *your basic behavior in this area is probably not going to change much.* My bottom line truth, therefore, is this: Rather than change your *behavior* to fit your *house,* change your *house* to fit your *behavior!*

I'm not saying you should never attempt to change bad habits or grow in your abilities as a housekeeper. I'm just saying there is a way to achieve a clean home *now* by approaching an old, familiar problem in a new, creative way.

Together we'll...

- evaluate the causes behind the cleaning problems in your home

- find solutions for these problems and create a workable plan to implement them
- explore your unique shortcomings when it comes to cleaning and how to work around them
- eliminate clutter and convert your entire house, room by room, into a house that cleans itself
- stop future messes before they happen
- set up a simple, ongoing maintenance plan to keep your home clean for good

Are you ready to dive in? We'll get started right after I share a housekeeping moment submitted to me.

My Most Embarrassing Messy House Story

—A Bathroom Surprise—

BY LINDA P.

When I was first married, I thought my new husband would clean up after himself like my dad did, so I helpfully put cleaning supplies in the bathroom next to the mudroom where he kept his farm clothes. I rarely if ever looked in that bathroom, assuming that he was taking care of it.

One fall day, about a week after they'd been planting wheat on the farm, I peeked in there and saw something odd. I ventured in to take a closer look and realized that seed wheat must have fallen out of my husband's coveralls, landed on the warm, wet bath mat, and germinated. By the time I discovered it, there was wheat almost four inches high growing from the bath mat!

Part 1

Get Ready...

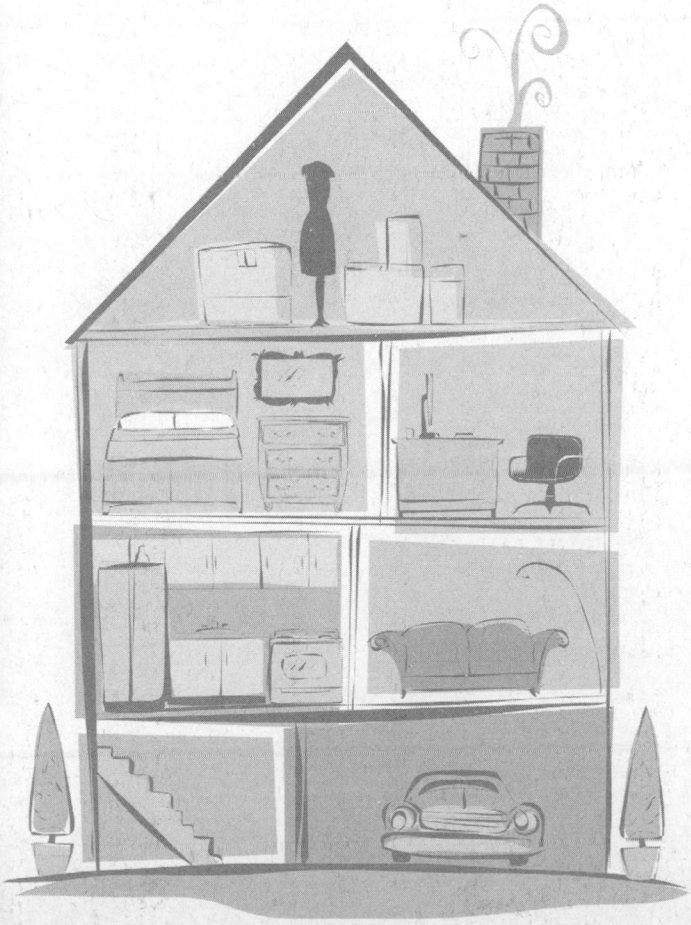

Step 1

Draw a Floor Plan and Determine Flow Pattern

In my Father's house are many rooms; if it were not so, I would have told you. I am going there to prepare a place for you. And if I go and prepare a place for you, I will come back and take you to be with me that you also may be where I am.

JOHN 14:2-3

The first step in your home's transformation is to get a fresh, clean spiral notebook. You'll be using this notebook throughout your house transformation, so choose one with a brightly colored cover so it won't get lost in the mess. With a marker, write in big letters on the cover "HTCI." This is your "House That Cleans Itself" notebook from now on.

For now, set the marker aside and grab a pencil with an eraser. It's time to do some drawing. (If you'd rather make the following sketches on plain white paper or on your computer and then staple them into your notebook that's okay too.) Whether you have any artistic or architectural ability or not, you should be able to sketch a bird's-eye view of your home and property. Try to keep it to scale as much as possible (for example, don't make the bathroom twice as big as the kitchen unless it really is), but don't make yourself crazy trying to get it perfect. What you want is a *working plan* to guide you through the conversion process, not a work of art.

As you sketch, include rudimentary shapes to represent the largest pieces of furniture, such as the dining table and your beds. Be sure to include windows and doors. Sketch each floor of your house separately, and don't forget to include attic and basement.

Once the drawing of your house is finished, add the exterior areas to the picture of your first floor, and be sure to include your driveway, front yard, front porch, garage, shed, back porch, deck, backyard, and whatever else constitutes the full extent of your property. As you add the outside spaces, exterior plantings are not necessary to include, other than the biggest trees and shrub lines. Again, you don't want to waste too much time on this or worry about making it perfect. Just get it done.

Now draw some rectangles to represent your car(s). You didn't think your car was going to escape the House That Cleans Itself System, did you?

Here's a sample floor plan:

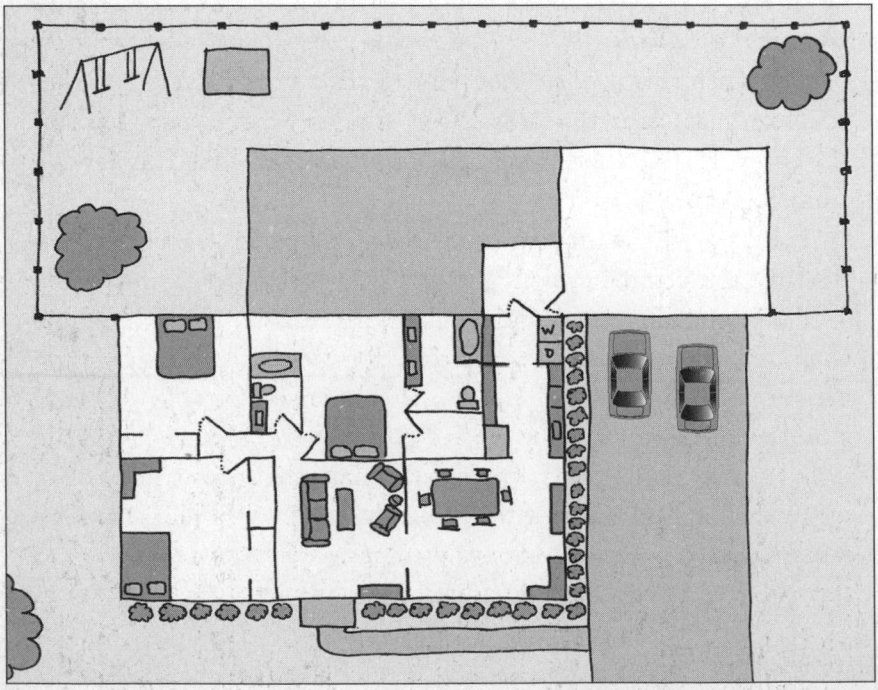

At this point, you may want to duplicate your drawing on a copy machine before you go any further in case yours gets messy as you work through the next steps.

Define Your Spaces

On your drawing, locate the entrance that is most commonly used by the greatest number of people. More than likely, this will be the front or side door. Using a fat marker, draw a circle or square or other shape that defines the space that is stepped into when coming through this entrance. In other words, whether your entrance opens into a formal foyer or a mud room or a kitchen or a living room or whatever, outline the room or the part of that room that you consider the primary "in and out" area of the home. Once you have defined that area, write "#1" inside.

Next, use your marker to outline all other rooms and/or areas in your plan as shown on the next page. Your goal is to define and delineate the various spaces in your house. For example, you would draw a line around the walls of your bathroom and another around your laundry room. If you have a desk in the corner of your dining room that you use as a home office, the area on your house plan that illustrates your dining room would have two shapes, one representing the "dining" part of the room and one representing the "office" part of the room.

You don't need to break things down too specifically; most rooms should be represented by a single shape because they serve one primary function. For large external spaces, think in terms of how the space is used. You might draw a line around your back porch or deck or patio, a line around your shed, and one around the yard. If your yard gets a lot of use and has distinct "zones," you might want to get more specific and indicate separate areas for the kids' swingset/sandbox area, your garden, and the grassy areas that are left. Don't forget to draw a rectangle around each of your cars.

When you are finished defining the spaces in and out of your home, it's time to choose the order you are going to purge, clean, and convert the areas to the House That Cleans Itself way of living.

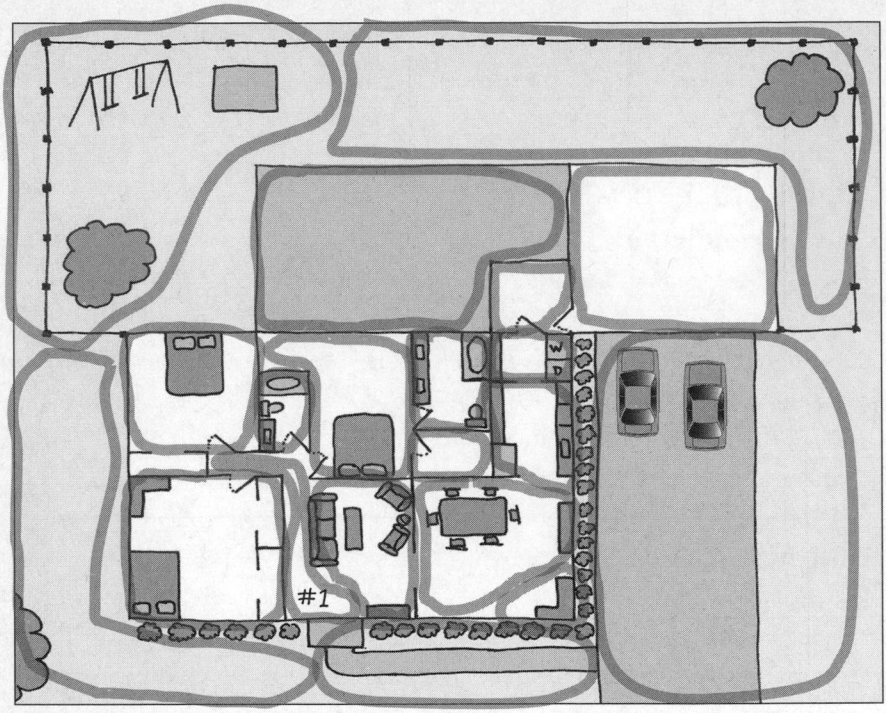

Determine Your Flow Pattern

Only you can know which parts of your home are in the most desperate need of help or are the most important to you. There's already a #1 written on your primary entry space, and that is where you are going to begin.

Before you number the other areas, read the rest of this chapter and the next one for inportant suggestions and considerations. Your goal in numbering areas is to lay out a "Flow Pattern" that makes sense to you and how you want to proceed through your home in this cleaning process.

The full HTCI conversion process might take a while, so you'll want to focus on the more public zones first, such as the kitchen and family room. On the other hand, if there is a less public area that's gotten totally out of control and is hindering your day-to-day life, such as a master bedroom or home office, then by all means number that area with a #2. Consider also your external spaces. If you're near a change of season, you may want to number the outside areas first or last, depending on whether it might be getting warmer or colder in the weeks ahead. Ditto for your attic or garage.

Be sure to read the nest chapter first to learn about your "Home Base Zone" to decide where it should fall in the numbering order.

One final thought as to how you number your spaces: If there is a *really* big job, such as a disastrous basement or attic, and there is no urgent need to clear it out soon, number that area last. Mess is still mess wherever it is, but taking the less-intimidating, more visible jobs first helps you keep going because you can feel and see your progress more readily.

When you are ready, assign a number to *every* area—inside and out—that has been defined on your plan. If you have no preference as to the order that these spaces are attacked, number them as you would move room to room in the most efficient, logical progression, as shown.

Congratulations! You are ready now to move on to the next step.

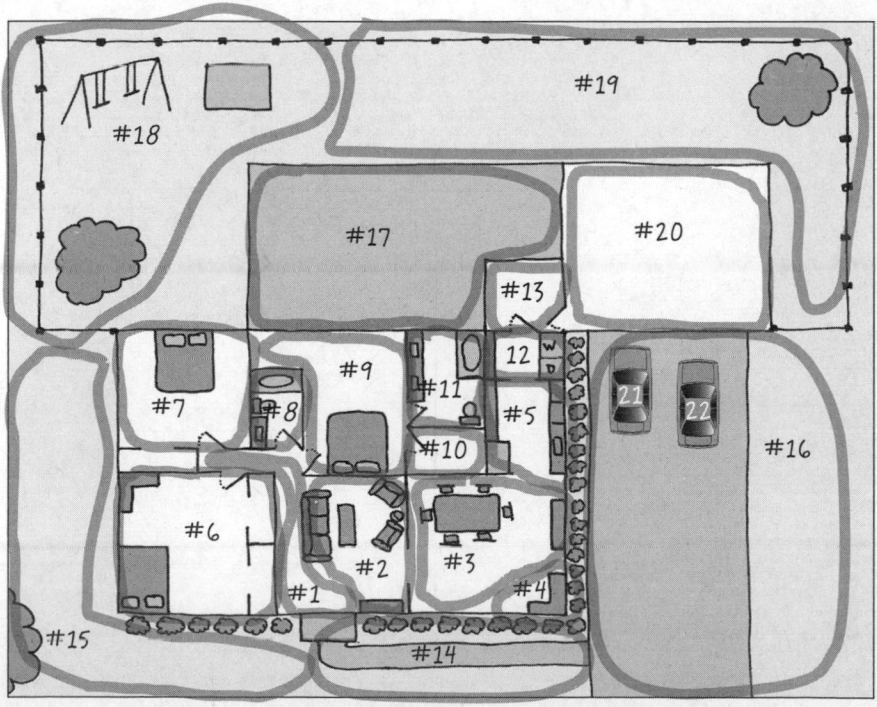

My Most Embarrassing Messy House Story

—My Not-So-Secret Clutter—

BY BERNARD B.

In transition between apartments, I once rented a bedroom in the large home of a friend. With full kitchen and living room privileges, I was careful to clean up after myself out there, particularly since the homeowner was a super-neat freak. I was much less careful in the bedroom I was using, where I tended to let things get out of hand.

One day I came home earlier than expected to find a crowd of neighbors hovering in the hallway outside my room, looking inside. The homeowner was with them, but when he spotted me, he looked guilty, like he'd been caught red-handed.

"What's going on?" I asked.

When no one answered, the little girl from across the street piped up. "He's letting people come see how messy your room is. He does it all the time."

Step 2

Decide on Your Home Base Zone

I have no peace, no quietness;
I have no rest, but only turmoil.

Job 3:26

Years ago when my kids were small and money was tight, we lived for a while in an old house that had almost no closets, an unusable basement, and very little in the way of storage. Most of the time mess was everywhere. I couldn't get a handle on my time, my organization, my clutter, or my cleaning. Consequently, I felt frustrated and discouraged much of the time.

At that time a wise friend sensed my desperation and offered some advice that I have used to this day: *When you can't get a handle on anything else in your house, figure out that one place that most affects you emotionally, clean it up, and keep it clean no matter what.* She said that everyone has someplace in their home that is important to them in a unique way, and when it's clean they feel an inordinate amount of satisfaction, and when it's dirty they feel an inordinate amount of irritation and stress.

Do you know what that place might be for you?

For Martha Cilley, the Internet's household-wisdom-dispensing "FlyLady," that area is her kitchen sink (check out www.flylady.net). Cilley's entire housekeeping makeover, in fact, begins with her directive to get into your kitchen, clean your sink, and keep it sparkling. While I agree with her idea in theory, I suggest that one woman's sink may be another woman's toilet. Only *you* can know what that one thing is in your home that most brings you peace if it's kept spotless. It may be your kitchen sink, but it may be something entirely different.

For me, I finally decided that special place was the upstairs bathroom. For some reason I'll never be able to explain, when that room was strewn with wet towels and dirty clothes and in need of a good scrubbing and mopping, I felt overwhelmed beyond comprehension. Conversely, on those rare occasions in the past when I had attacked that room with vigor and made it sparkle, I felt strangely calm and proud. Sometimes when it was clean, I would even stand in the doorway just to look at it and feel happy.

My wise friend was right. Following her advice, I made that little bathroom my cleaning priority. Sure enough, even when the whole house was a cluttered mess from one end to the other, as long as that bathroom was neat and clean, I knew all was not lost.

When I developed and refined the HTCI System, I dubbed this special sanity-saving area the "Home Base Zone" (HBZ). You may not realize it, but you have an HBZ in your home too. To figure out where yours is, think about what bothers you the most when it's a mess and makes you the happiest when it's clean.

Linda describes the search for her HBZ:

> When I heard about the Home Base Zone concept, it took a long time for me to identify my zone. I knew it wasn't the upstairs bathroom. I tried Cilley's FlyLady advice, but it definitely wasn't the kitchen sink. Then one day a very naturally neat friend made the comment that she never allowed herself to put anything on her closet floors or under her bed.
>
> I was stunned. Nothing on the closet floor? Nothing under the bed? But what about all that wasted storage space? What about all those things that have nowhere else to go?

In reply she suggested I take a look at my own bedroom closet floor and under my own bed. Chances are, she told me, the few things placed there intentionally as "storage" were surrounded on all sides by mess, dust, and dirt.

She was 100 percent right.

I knew I had found my new Home Base Zone. With a strange lightness, I spent the next day—and it took all day—cleaning out my closet and under my bed. I weeded out everything I didn't need—all the clothes and shoes that had gone out of style or didn't fit and all the needless little items I had tucked away for "later." Later was here, and I still didn't need them. The underbed storage boxes? Gone. They held our off-season clothing, so I couldn't get rid of them entirely. I relegated them to a different place in a different room. Yes, I did sacrifice some storage area under my bed. But the feeling it gives me to know that it is clean and empty under there is worth the trade-off.

When my purge and organization were finished, the only items left without a "place" were my shoes. Wanting to keep the closet floor clear, I bought two hanging shoe bags for $7 each at the local discount store, hung them from the rod, and placed each of my pairs of shoes in the little cubbyholes. Not only were the shoes off the floor, but now I was able to see them better, retrieve them more easily, and I no longer had to scrounge around in the dark recesses of the closet, feeling under fallen clothes and among other shoes and boots for a lost mate.

When all of my purging and organization was complete and the floor of my closet and under the bed were clear, I vacuumed and mopped away dust that had accumulated to an alarming amount. (In fact there was so much dust under the bed that I actually made myself sick by stirring it all up. For the next week a stuffy nose and stopped-up head reminded me that I had been sleeping directly over that dust for a long time, never wondering what it might be doing to my health.)

For the first time in a while, I had defined and cleaned my Home Base Zone. I have kept it clean and clutter free ever since. Honestly, it doesn't matter to anyone on this earth except me that there's nothing under my bed, not even a dust bunny. But that knowledge brings me joy, and that's what matters. Until it was completely clean, I didn't realize how much subconscious stress my messy, dusty closet and underbed areas gave me. But now that they are clean, that stress has been converted into a strange and reassuring peace.

Getting into Your Zone

How about you? Where's your HBZ? Answers vary widely, from a single shelf to an entire room. An online pole netted the following responses:

- my bed—as long as the bed is made, I'm happy
- my kitchen
- the counter by the back door
- the inside of my car
- my shed
- the part of the basement that we use as a pantry
- the front porch
- the kitchen floor—I can't stand to have a dirty or sticky kitchen floor
- my home office
- the toilets in all the bathrooms
- the area that surrounds my easy chair in the den
- the part of the laundry room where everybody dumps stuff when they come in the back door

As you can see, there is no right answer, except the answer that's right for you. If you can't think of where your Home Base Zone might be, ask your family to venture some guesses. Chances are, one of them might be able to tell you what you haven't been able to figure out yourself.

Purge and Clean That Zone

Once you know what and where your HBZ is, the next step is to completely strip it of all unnecessary items. In a later chapter, I'll be teaching you how to purge clutter from your house. For now, it's enough that you get the unnecessary stuff out of your HBZ. I recommend that you put the stuff into a cardboard box and carry that box to another room. The point is to *get every single thing that doesn't belong* out of that zone.

Once all the extras are gone, move everything that *does* belong out of the way and scrub your HBZ until it shines. No, I'm not kidding. In a book that's supposed to tell you how to get your house to clean itself, I am suggesting that you get down on your hands and knees and do some deep cleaning the old-fashioned way. Depending on what and where your zone is, that can mean vacuuming, wiping, mopping, hosing off, and/or hand scrubbing. Whatever it takes, clean your zone as thoroughly as possible. When you are finished, put back the items that belong in a neat and orderly fashion. Use effective, logical storage solutions as needed. If you purchase any new organizational tools such as bins or trays, do so only after measuring the available area for a perfect fit. Only buy these types of material when needed for specific needs.

Now that you have defined your HBZ, purged it of everything except what absolutely has to be there, cleaned it until it shines, and restocked it, you are well on your way to losing your messy-house guilt, freeing up your time, and transforming your house and your life.

Make the commitment to keep your Home Base Zone looking

clean and neat, even if everything else in your home feels like it's falling apart. Believe it or not, that sense of peace and control this gives you will soon spread to the other parts of your home!

My Most Embarrassing Messy House Story

—Capturing the Moment—

BY CORINNE Z.

My child's birthday party brought much work—closets to clean, floors to scrub, clutter to hide. Hours later I had conquered it all. (I have this bizarre compulsion to clean everything if I'm going to clean anything.) The closets, gleaming and organized, brought tears of satisfaction to my eyes.

Until my father wandered in. According to him, the moment was so rare that he wanted to capture it on film. He ran back and got the video camera, and then he returned and began filming. In awe, he traveled from room to room, immortalizing the cleanliness on film—all the while quipping sarcastic commentary.

Sigh. At least he noticed it was clean.

Step 3

Involve the Household and Hang the Signs

My people will live in peaceful dwelling places, in secure homes, in undisturbed places of rest.

Isaiah 32:18

If you live alone, you can skip this step—though you might want to give a heads-up to the cat or dog. But if you live with a spouse and/or kids and/or other family members and/or roommates, you need to bring everyone on board. Talk to your spouse (or other adults in the house) first, and then form a unified front as you round up the kids for a meeting.

Ask them how they feel about the current mess, disorganization, division of chores, and so forth. Leave your defenses at the door and be ready to hear some uncomfortable words. Uncontrolled mess has a greater impact on family members than most of us want to believe. For many years, no one understood the dangers of secondhand smoke. Offices were filled with it, restaurants, even airplanes. Nonsmokers had to put up with it. Then researchers began to see a correlation between smoking and cancer and even secondhand smoke and cancer. The more they studied, the more they realized that a person could get lung cancer simply by living in close proximity to a smoker. The cancer of a messy, chaotic house is lethal in its own way too, and not just to the one who is most responsible for the mess.

Hear the pain in these comments made by adults who grew up amid mess:

> *"I was never allowed to bring friends home because the house wasn't clean enough."*
>
> *"Our house was always filthy except when we had out-of-town company visit, then my mom would go crazy cleaning everything! She cleaned the backs of closets those people were never going to see."*
>
> *"My homework was ruined more than once when I set it down on the table only to find out too late that there was a puddle of liquid there left from dinner the night before!"*
>
> *"My parents fought constantly about the mess."*
>
> *"My mother was so busy cleaning all the time, but she never seemed to get anywhere."*

What household chaos really boils down to is lack of structure. People who grow up without structure tend to be very creative and spontaneous, which are good things. But they also can be irresponsible, undisciplined, and, if other factors are present, prone to addiction because they learn early on how to fill that craving for structure with something else.

Need more evidence that the state of your home impacts your children? According to a study done by the University of Michigan and presented at the 2001 annual meeting of the American Economic Association, kids who are raised in clean homes are more likely to complete more school and have higher earning potential than those raised in dirty homes. That fact doesn't surprise me. The stress of dirt and/or extreme mess can be highly destructive to everyone who lives in it.

As you discuss your plans with your children, if they bring up terms like "frustration" or "embarrassment," don't feel bad. In fact, be glad! You've got them right where you want them. Dissatisfaction with the status quo is a wonderful impetus for change. Explain to them that you've been frustrated with the house too, but together all of you can turn the situation around 180 degrees.

What if everyone in your house *except you* thinks your home is more than clean enough already? Then pause and consider whether it's your standards, rather than your home, that need help. If so, then tone down your goals accordingly. Sometimes we have a skewed view of how clean our homes should be. If that's the case, implementing a more ambitious plan than you need will cause unnecessary work and aggravation for all involved.

In any event, try to help everyone in the house capture your vision for change or, at the very least, agree not to be an impediment. No matter what they tell you, never underestimate how important basic cleanliness and structure are to children and spouses. As a child I couldn't even put my finger on what it was about Mary Poppins' self-cleaning room that filled me with such yearning. But as an adult, what I have come to understand is that I didn't just want an end to a messy bedroom, I wanted *an end to the feeling of chaos* that living in that kind of chaos produced.

Decide not to live that way any longer. You, your spouse, and your children deserve much better than that.

What can you say or do if your family doesn't want to embrace the HTCI System?

If Your Family Resists...

Some of the most common objections I've heard from individuals, couples, and kids follow. I've included some suggested responses you can use or adapt to fit your situation.

"I'm afraid you'll put too many demands on me, and I'm overloaded already."

Tell them that what you need primarily is their emotional support and cooperation. Let them know you respect their schedules and commitments and won't overload them. Remind them that in the long run, having a house that cleans itself will *lessen* everyone's burdens around the house and free up more time, sometimes quite significantly.

"I'm afraid you intend to spend a lot of money on this, money we don't have."

The HTCI System can be implemented with little or no expense. Promise to make only the no-cost or low-cost changes at first, and if you reach a point where you feel that an expenditure would greatly help the process, discuss it at that time and decide together whether it's worth it or not.

Remember too how much money is wasted because of disorganization and mess. Have you ever added up late fees to the video store and the library, discounts you didn't take advantage of because you responded too late, coupons you cut out and never found again, lost checks and cash—not to mention the cost of your time? Unless you're talking about hiring a butler, *living messy costs much more than living neatly,* especially if you have to bring in a weekly cleaning service to stay on top of things.

"This plan won't work."

Arranging your house in a logical manner so that it more readily stays clean will always work. If this is their objection, press further to find out what they're really saying.

When Janey decided to implement the House That Cleans Itself System, she was surprised to meet opposition from her entire family. For the kids, they simply saw it as more chores. But as Janey described her goals, casting her vision of less mess, more free time, rewards for success, and less stress on everyone, they began to get on board.

If your children or teens are still objecting, it may be because they don't really understand how the system works or they fear it will mean more hassle for them. Let them express those thoughts. Then gently attempt to bring them around to the HTCI System.

Whatever you do, don't announce the plan and dictate how they should feel about it. Instead, describe the plan in terms of their specific hopes, issues, and needs.

For example, remind them of the field trip they had to miss because you lost the permission slip and didn't send it in. Tell them that by creating a house that cleans itself, you'll be able to keep better track of all of your papers so that hopefully nothing like that will happen again.

Remind your preteen of how she felt when her friends came over to spend the night and saw that a bunch of her dirty clothes had made their way under the bed. Tell her that with a house that cleans itself, you're going to block off the underside of her bed with wood slats so that can't happen anymore.

You shouldn't bring up past hurts to manipulate your children into doing what you want them to do, of course, but sometimes kids need reminding about obstacles from the past so they can see real, tangible value in your plans for the future. Done compassionately, this sort of conversation can be very effective.

When it came to her husband, Janey had a bigger challenge. He'd spent 11 years of marriage watching her try to get their home clean and organized. She'd always failed in the past; he wasn't about to get his hopes up this time. I suggested she tell him to allow her actions to speak louder than her words. "Tell him not to invest emotionally in your grand scheme," I said. "Ask him to cooperate, to be a team player in front of the kids, and to not be an obstructionist."

She did as I suggested, and he grudgingly agreed. It took a while, but after about four months, he finally admitted that things seemed different around their house, much more in control. Once he showed that little spark of hope, she was able to take him around the house and point out changes she'd made, explaining the thinking behind them and the ways those little changes were having a big impact on the amount of time she spent cleaning. After that he jumped in with both feet and even set about making some of the bigger changes she wanted. Together they put in some new flooring, a Sight Zone concealer wall, and even some wall-mounted lighting fixtures. In the end, he was a full convert to the House That Cleans Itself way of living. He hadn't wanted to get his hopes up, but in the end his hopes were realized. By then he was even more sold on the process than she was.

Whatever your family's objections, remember that you can always pull from this books bits and pieces of good advice and information rather than do an entire household conversion. If your family simply will not budge, keep implementing the ideas in this book. Numerous small touches around your home will add up to a lot, reducing the burden of housekeeping for you and your family.

Hang the Signs

One of my favorite sayings is, "You've got to break a lot of eggs to bake a cake." My friend, you are about to break some eggs. For a while, maybe for a month or more, your house is going to look worse, not better, than it does right now. Think you can stand it? Think you'll just die of shame if someone drops by while you're "under construction"?

That's why I've included a sign you can tear out or make photocopies from. It warns visitors that you are under construction with the HTCI System. If you have even the slightest hesitation about breaking eggs in your house as you begin to enact some of these changes, put copies of this sign at the entrance and exit to whatever area you are working on.

Go ahead. Hang the sign(s). If you have kids, let them help you so they'll feel part of the process from the very beginning.

When your new neighbor stops by to borrow a cup of sugar and you're knee-deep in the clutter you just pulled out of the front hall closet, you'll thank me.

PLEASE PARDON OUR MESS!

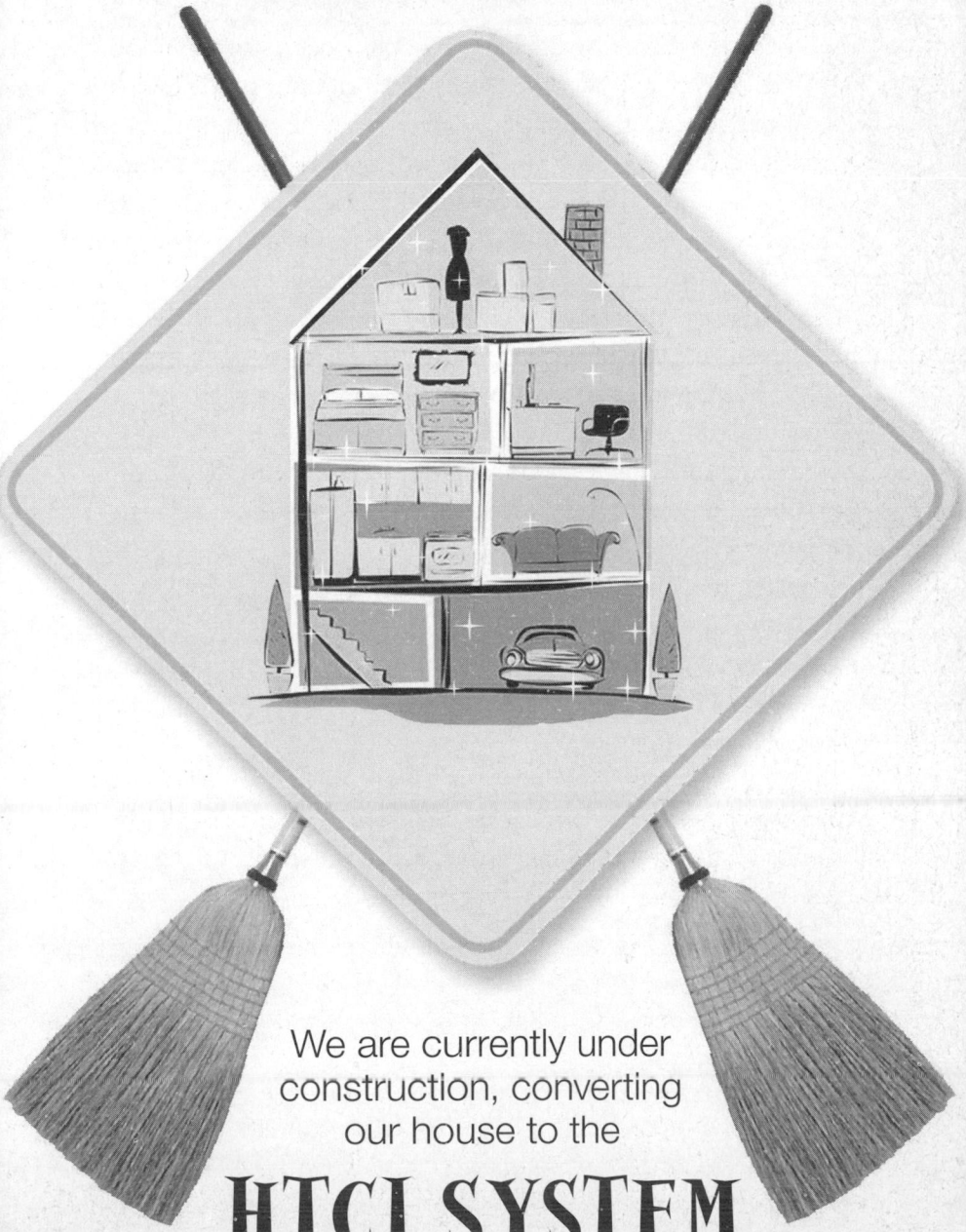

We are currently under construction, converting our house to the

HTCI SYSTEM

My Most Embarrassing Messy House Story

—Vacation from Cleaning—

BY JUSTINE M.

Our friends used to loan us their vacation house in the mountains. We'd go there often for long weekends with our two small children. About halfway through one such weekend, I was getting tired of waiting on everyone hand and foot, so I declared a strike. After all, it was *my* vacation too! I didn't cook or do dishes. Soon the sink was piled high with dirty dishes, the entire house was a mess from one end to the other, and toys and clothes were strewn everywhere.

On our last night there we decided to go out to eat, get a good night's sleep, and attack the mess first thing in the morning. We would be leaving the next day anyway, so one more night of mess wasn't going to hurt anything...or so we thought.

Unfortunately, there was a slight mix-up about our timing. Thinking we had left that afternoon, the owners decided to start their own vacation a few days early.

They arrived while we were at the restaurant, and when we got back to the house, their car was parked outside. I nearly died. It would have been one thing to let my own house go, but it was quite another to do it to someone else's—and then have them see it that way before we were able to clean it back up!

They were incredibly gracious about it and never seemed to doubt that we would restore the home to its former pristine condition, which of course we did right then and as quickly as possible. But I've never gotten over the shame of being caught in such a mess.

Step 4

Put God at the Center

Commit to the LORD whatever you do,
and your plans will succeed.

PROVERBS 16:3

At this point, you should have an HTCI notebook, a numbered floor plan, a family fully on board, a sign hanging in your entryway that announces your house is "under construction," and a spotlessly clean Home Base Zone. You're probably starting to feel hopeful and maybe even a little excited! Are you ready to jump in with both feet?

Well, there's one more crucial step to put into place before the work of the HTCI System is implemented. We need to take a moment to put your home's upcoming transformation into God's hands and make him the center of your housecleaning efforts. That may sound a bit odd, but going on a "prayer walk" of your home will help you find the focus, strength, and encouragement to start, persevere, and complete the HTCI System.

Prayer Walk Your House

Have you ever heard of "prayer walking"? That's where you take a stroll through a neighborhood or town while praying for the people in each home or business as you go by. My church strongly supports prayer walking to bathe our entire region in prayer. They even have a map of our county on which we can place pins on the streets we cover during our regular walks.

I've done plenty of prayer walking in my neighborhood, but only when I decided to get a handle on our mess and clutter did it cross my mind to prayer walk my *house.* I highly encourage you to begin the House That Cleans Itself process with an indoor prayer walk of your own. It will focus your efforts, reaffirm your priorities, and give you the opportunity to ask for God's blessings upon you and your family in very specific ways. If you've never prayer walked before, you may feel a little silly doing it at first, but do it anyway. Soon you'll be lost in the prayer itself, and your self-consciousness will fly out the window.

Just be sure that this is one prayer you give with your eyes open—lest you trip over the mess you want to clean up.

Preparing for Your Prayer Walk

Before you begin, there are a few matters to consider.

Should you do it alone or with your family? I first thought my prayer walk would be a family event, but when I mentioned it at dinner one night, I was met with blank stares and uncomfortable shrugs. My family's not usually shy on prayer, but something about going through our home and praying for each room in turn didn't appeal to them as it did to me. They thought it sounded kind of...well...odd.

I finally decided that for me cleaning isn't just a responsibility; it's also a mission. I needed to prayer walk my house to put God at the center of my housecleaning mission. I did the prayer walk alone. As it turned out, the time was more intense, focused, unhurried, and pleasing than it might have been had my family shared in the experience.

Talk to your family and see what they want to do. Whether the prayer walk is done in a family group or you do it alone, it will be an uplifting, encouraging experience.

Choose a time that won't be interrupted. Take the phone off the hook, turn off all cell phones, and prepare to have quiet and peace for at least 30 minutes. If you have small children at home, don't do this while they are underfoot. Send them on an outing with a babysitter, relative, or friend. If that's not possible, at the very least, wait until they are sound asleep.

Heed the words of Matthew 5:23-24: "Therefore, if you are offering your gift at the altar and there remember that your brother has something against you, leave your gift there in front of the altar. First go and be reconciled to your brother; then come and offer your gift." If you know there are issues in your life that need to be taken care of, do so now *before* you begin so your time with God is not hindered.

Use your Flow Plan. Let the numbered floor plan you drew in Step 1 determine the place you begin and the order you take your walk. You want to bathe your entire home and outside areas in prayer. Following that order will mean nothing is left out.

As you take your prayer walk, ask God to show you the perfect place to set up a devotional area. If you already have a regular devotional routine that works for you, skip this point. But if you keep putting "have devotional time" on your to-do list (or as one of your New Year's Resolutions) but don't get around to it nearly often enough, this step is vital. When you get to Step 9, you'll learn to identify and eliminate what I call "Rabbit Trails"—all the places you have to go to gather materials you need to perform a specific task—but this is the most important Rabbit Trail to eliminate. Somewhere in your home is a place where you can grab some quiet moments on a daily basis to read God's Word and pray. When your prayer walk is over, the very next step you take will be to set up this devotional area so you can take on this new habit and easily make it part of each and every day.

How to Prayer Walk a House

If you have never prayer walked before, you're probably wondering how it works. Prayer walking outside is done very discreetly, a sort of silent, running prayer to God in your mind as you walk through a neighborhood or down a city street. A prayer walk through your home, however, can be quite a different experience. Because no one is looking or listening, feel free to pray out loud, pause in different places as you feel led, raise your hands, recite scripture, even burst into song or dance to the Lord. Afraid you'll feel stupid? Please don't! This is between you and God, and he treasures your transparency and willingness to come to him this way.

Let's start by going to the place you marked on your Flow Plan as #1, which should be just inside the main doorway. Pause there, close your eyes, and allow the quiet to envelop you. This is your time with the Lord. Don't rush it.

Start by simply praising God. Recite a psalm of praise, or sing a refrain of "Our God Is an Awesome God," or just speak to him with reverence and appreciation. You might read some psalms or other praise verses aloud, such as this verse from Revelation 4:11: "You are worthy, our Lord and God, to receive glory and honor and power, for you created all things, and by your will they were created and have their being."

Next, still in that same place, confess any sin that may be coming between you and your Maker. Ask God for forgiveness and allow him to cleanse your heart. Isn't God's grace amazing? Rejoice!

Tell God how much you want to honor him through the keeping of your home. Ask him to bless your house and all who live in it. Give each family member to him by name, perhaps reciting Joshua 24:15: "Choose for yourselves this day whom you will serve...But as for me and my household, we will serve the LORD." Ask God to shine his light through you and yours to all who pass through this doorway.

Now open your eyes and look around this area and pray aloud any specific concerns that you have regarding its organization or cleanliness. For example, you might say, "Please help me find a way to keep everyone from dumping their sports equipment right here on the floor" or "Please help me keep from feeling resentful when my husband leaves his briefcase there on the counter." You don't need to make a laundry list of everything that's wrong with the room, but for any specific issues that pop into your head, go ahead and commit them to prayer. The God who knows the exact number of hairs on your head is happy to hear about and help with your most mundane household struggles.

Continue praying as you move to the next area on your Flow Plan. Beyond any specifics, you can ask for help in keeping the home clean, in maintaining focus and structure, in reinforcing habits, in maintaining discipline. Ask also that the Lord help you see your trouble spots and give you ideas for how best to handle them. Ask for patience, respect, and discernment in dealing with family members as they join you in your quest for cleanliness.

If you reach an area and no words come to mind, sing a hymn or recite a scripture instead. As you work through your Flow Plan, when you reach the outside areas of your home such as your yard, shed, or car, if those areas don't afford any privacy, you'll probably want to remain inside at a window and look out as you pray. If going outside and discreetly continuing your prayer walk won't disrupt the "flow" and cause you to get distracted, then by all means do so.

As you move throughout your home, bathing it in prayer, remember to be thankful and to keep a grateful heart for all your material blessings. That we have been blessed with a house and possessions to get messy in the first place is something we often forget.

Finally, remember to ask God to keep you mindful of the main priority here, that you get past the mess so you can free yourself to be the person God want's you to be. End your prayer walk by asking that he plant in you enthusiasm and energy for the HTCI process and how you can serve him more once your home is under control. With that vision in your mind, it's easier not to get bogged down by the work that lies ahead.

Why Prayer Walk

Besides placing your petitions for help before the Lord, my hope is that the prayer walk will change your heart by reminding you that God's hand is on your entire home, messy or clean, under control or out of control, and that his love and his purpose covers all of your shortcomings. Romans 8:31 asks, "If God is for us, who can be against us?" Truly, God is *for* you, and he wants to help you put house cleaning in its proper place—no more and no less important than it should be.

My Most Embarrassing Messy House Story

—A Corny Tale—

BY BETTY R.

I had gone to the trouble of boiling several ears of corn and slicing off the kernels to make a good-sized bowl of delicious, buttery, sweet corn. Because our Bible study members wouldn't be arriving for the meal for another half hour, I put the bowl of corn in the microwave and hit the "keep warm" button. Our small group came for dinner. We enjoyed the chicken, mashed potatoes and gravy, biscuits, vegetable casserole, and dessert.

It wasn't until the next time I used the microwave—*five days later*—that I discovered the bowl of corn. All that work of cutting the kernels off those piping hot ears, and then I forgot to serve it. I was mad at myself for my absentmindedness—not to mention nauseated by the awful stench of five-day-old corn!

Step 5

Gather Tools and Document Evidence

If you accept my words and store up my commands within you, turning your ear to wisdom and applying your heart to understanding, and if you call out for insight and cry aloud for understanding, and if you look for it as for silver and search for it as for hidden treasure, then you will understand the fear of the LORD *and find the knowledge of God. For the* LORD *gives wisdom, and from his mouth come knowledge and understanding.*

PROVERBS 2:1-6

For years I thought that getting a house organized began with buying lots of cool holders, bins, dividers, and charts and then the stuff would almost jump inside and organize itself. I didn't know I should never buy any organizational product unless it serves a specific function in a specific place. And even then the purchase should be made only after I've measured for it and determined the exact size and shape of organizer I need. In fact, it wasn't until I began researching housekeeping in earnest that I learned that *most organizational products create more mess than they help to contain.*

Think, for example, of your desk area, that place where you do paperwork. How many desktop sorters do you own? I'm talking about those multipurpose holders designed to keep pens, paper clips, and such neatly contained and easily within reach. Right now does your desk look like it did in the photo that came with it when you bought it?

Probably not. In truth, when we have sorters and dividers and cubbies and containers, we messy folks will either fill the various areas with all sorts of junk that just makes a bigger mess or we ignore the various compartments completely and heap guilt on ourselves for not using them like we "should."

Allow me to free you from your guilt. I urge you to avoid most holders entirely. The very *last* step in any organizational process is to buy the holders or other products you need. First sort, purge, measure, and see if you can use something else you already have on hand. So if you were planning a trip to the store in the next few days to buy a variety of containers, let me put your mind at rest. The tools you need in the beginning are not at all what you're expecting.

Here's what you do need to get started:

- a *step ladder or tall stool* you can easily carry from room to room
- a *camera,* preferably digital, so you can see your photos right away
- a *pen or pencil* and your *HTCI notebook,* which contains the Flow Plan you created in *Step 1*

Accumulating Evidence

If you stopped neatening your house altogether—and I mean avoiding even the smallest gesture like picking up a wayward sock—how long would it take for it to fall apart? How long before the detritus of life would begin to accumulate in various places on the floor or tables? How long before the counters and floors would get too cluttered to use? Or is your house already a disaster, and you're half expecting the health department to come calling any minute?

Either way, this may be one of the few times in life where having a messy house is an advantage. If most of your house is a mess *right now,* jump down to the next section, *"Time to Document,"* and keep reading. If your house is fairly clean right now, stick with me here, as my next suggestion may sound a bit odd.

Stop cleaning. If your house is neat right now, that's exactly what I want you to do. Hang the sign from *Step 3,* if need be, and refrain from *all housework* except for feeding your family and staying on top of the dirty dishes. You can do a load of laundry if you absolutely have to. But otherwise, live your normal life without any straightening, without any cleaning, and especially without picking up after anyone else. Don't intentionally be a slob and leave stuff out just for the fun of it, but don't clean up after yourself any more than you ordinarily would on your worst or laziest or busiest day.

More than likely, a day or two of noncleaning will suffice, and then you can move on to the next part. (On the other hand, if you can go ten days and the place still looks great, either someone else is picking up without your knowledge or you've already got such wonderful systems in place that this book will only provide insights into new ways to do cleaning.) When your house has reached the point you call "messy," you're ready to move on to "Time to Document."

Time to Document

Have you ever wanted to be a cop or a private detective? Here's your chance. You are now on a mission to collect clues throughout your home. What you're looking for is evidence of where, when, and why stuff accumulates in the way that it does.

Primarily you need to zero in on the problem areas and problem habits in your house. You probably expect junk to pile up in certain places—shoes near the front door, magazines or newspapers beside the sofa, clothes tossed over a chair in your bedroom. But beyond the items you expect to see, I want you to consider the ones you don't expect. More than likely they are a big part of what's tripping up your daily housekeeping efforts.

It's human nature to stop seeing what's in front of us all the time.

That's why you're going to use a stool and a camera to find new perspectives on familiar spaces. You'll use the notebook to record your findings.

Starting at area #1 as defined in your Flow Plan, take a look around and write down every housekeeping issue you see in that area. For example, in your notebook you might write:

Area #1

- shoes lying around on floor
- papers for school shoved on table
- car keys in a heap on counter
- library books and video rentals piled by door
- backpacks and gym bags everywhere
- sports equipment scattered on floor
- gloves and scarves on table

When you've written down everything you can, climb up the stepladder, look down from a bird's-eye view, and see if you notice anything else. For example:

- dirty footprints by door
- doormat askew and looks messy
- fingerprints all over mirror beside door
- plant in corner wilting from lack of water

While you're up there, snap a photo or two to record the entire area on film. Now climb down and move on to the area designated as #2 on your Flow Plan.

Repeat the process, keeping in mind that you aren't just making a list of the specific items that are messing up that room or area right now, you're also looking for the *types* of problems that are cropping up there as well. For example, in the lists I just mentioned, it's obvious this home has no "in the door/out the door" system for corralling those things that were dumped by various household members on their way in or out of the home. So while cleaning a house would involve putting each of those wayward items where they belong, setting up a House That Cleans Itself would also involve identifying a logical, convenient place *nearby* for those items to go regularly.

Continue to work your way through your entire Flow Plan, climbing up on the stool, snapping photos, and writing down your findings as you do. One caveat: Skip three or four lines in your notebook between every single entry, and skip two or three pages between every separate area. More will be added in subsequent steps.

Once you've made your way through your entire place, you're ready to move on to the next step.

My Most Embarrassing Messy House Story

—More Than Meets the Eye—

BY JENNY R.

I decided to surprise my husband by preceding him home for lunch... and leaving a trail of clothing to the bedroom where I was waiting naked. But he brought his boss home with him and apologized for the messy house because he didn't get it. The boss did though...and made a quick exit!

The boss went to our church and always smiled at me with a twinkle in his eye after that. He also told my husband he'd give anything if his wife would do that sometime.

Step 6

Evaluate Evidence

For wisdom will enter your heart,
and knowledge will be pleasant to your soul.

PROVERBS 2:10

Once you have gathered your evidence from one end of your house to the other, including all external spaces, it's time to sit down and evaluate what you've learned. Download your photos or have them developed. Bring them to the table, along with the notes you made in your notebook. Study each picture in turn. More than likely you'll notice even more things about the mess than you did when you were making your rounds and snapping pictures. In your notebook, use some of those extra pages between areas to write down every single thing you didn't make note of before.

When Beverly reached this step, she was surprised to see in many of the photos at least one empty soda can. Her home recycle center is in the laundry room where eventually the cans went home to roost. But her photos showed that she had a more immediate problem: Until the cans made their way to the laundry room, they were cluttering up the entire house. Beverly's intentions were good (at least she didn't throw them in the trash), but she didn't think to take the cans every time she went into the laundry room. All it took to solve this problem was to put smaller "intermediate" recycling buckets (she used plastic dishpans) in several key areas but out of sight. Whenever one of those smaller containers gets full, she carries it to the main recycle bucket, dumps in the cans, and then returns the empty bin to where it belongs. This simple solution eliminated Beverly's problem of "can clutter."

Things to Watch For

As you study your photos and notes, here are some common examples of what you might find contributing to your clutter:

- groceries, especially bulk items, left on the kitchen counter
- coats and jackets left on the coat rack after the season is over
- interrupted projects left on tables
- jumbles of wires near computer and appliances
- magnets and papers cluttering up the front of fridge
- clothes worn once and hung from backs of chairs
- containers holding items that ought to go in cabinets or drawers or on shelves
- DVDs, videos, and games left on the floor near the television
- cleaning products left out where they were used
- stuff piled on the floor because it has nowhere else to go
- stuff piled at bottom of stairs waiting to go up, or at the top of the stairs waiting to come down
- "extras" of items currently being used: purses, curling irons or straighteners, uniforms, jackets
- exercise equipment such as balls, rackets, and pads
- trash that didn't make it to the trash can

- items that need to be thrown away: empty pill bottles, boxes from mail, packaging from items purchased
- clean, folded clothes that need to be put away
- dirty clothes that need to be taken to laundry room
- damp bath towels no one will claim
- books and magazines you've finished reading
- stuff waiting to be given away or donated
- hoses left in a heap on the grass
- filled boxes or containers shoved in the garage for organizing later
- phone books and directories lying open where used
- holiday decorations you missed when you packed up from the last holiday (or the one before that)
- unswept leaves cluttering the back patio

In every case, your next step is to think about and write down the *root cause* of each problem listed, using the blank lines between entries. Don't think too hard, just jot down the first thought that comes to mind when you look at each item you've listed in your notebook. Using the previous list as a guide, you might write:

- groceries, especially bulk items, left on the kitchen counter—*Too tired to do it right after doing all that grocery shopping, then got busy with something else*
- coats and jackets left on the coat rack after the season is over—*Time got away from me, didn't notice they were still there*
- interrupted projects left on tables—*Thought for sure I'd get back to that pretty soon*
- jumbles of wires near computer and appliances—*Never noticed before*
- magnets and papers cluttering up front of fridge—*Those*

papers are important reminders and have to go somewhere that we can see them on a regular basis

- clothes worn once and hung from backs of chairs—*Don't want to hang them with clean clothes but not ready to toss them in dirty clothes either*

You get the idea. For every single messy area in your home, there is a knee-jerk response that provides a reason why it is that way. Go through your entire notebook and write down that response to *every single problem* on your list. Your evidence is coming together nicely, and you may already be thinking of ways to eliminate some of these root causes once and for all. You may also be noticing some bad habits that need to be faced and eliminated, though perhaps not in the ways you would expect.

Remember, the goal for a House That Cleans Itself is to change the house first, and then change the behavior only when absolutely necessary.

More Kinds of Messes

As you continue to catalog and analyze your evidence, there are three more types of messes you may not have noticed.

Barnacling

This is a term my husband and I coined years ago when we recognized our tendency to utilize every available horizontal surface to put stuff on, sometimes within moments of the surface's appearing. Anything from a TV tray to an old trunk—in other words, just about anything with a horizontal surface—soon gets covered with stuff. Much as a ship's hull will attract barnacles that latch on and stay, we tend to barnacle surfaces all over the house.

Does your family tend to barnacle as well? If so, make note of the horizontal surfaces in your home that should be kept clear and the ways in which they have been covered up.

Tinies

I'm not sure when this term evolved, but I use it to refer to those little items that show up in vast quantities all over the house—in drawers, boxes, baskets, and containers. Think pens, crayons, markers, buttons, paper clips, hair ties, Lego pieces, Barbie shoes, bobby pins, safety pins, washers, screws, picture hangers, pennies—whatever tiny items tend to get tossed into the nearest receptacle for putting somewhere better later.

Some organizational experts will tell you to purge this sort of minutia (except for the pennies) whenever you run across it. Rather than do that, I'm going to ask you to consolidate instead. When you begin doing your purge, you're going to bring along a container in which you will collect your Tinies. What you do with them after that will be explained at that time.

Mess Because of Mess

About 10 years ago, when Olga was trying to get a handle on the clutter in her house, she bought a bunch of rolling metal racks, the kind you hang clothes on. She placed a rack in each of her three spare bedrooms, which made it easy for her children and grandchildren to hang up their clothes whenever they came to visit. Slowly, however, between visits Olga began to use these racks to store clothes: extra clothes, out-of-season clothes, clothes she was ready to donate, clothes that didn't fit her anymore. Eventually the racks were full.

Most clutterers have trouble with the clothing issue, but in this case there was some real irony at work. The reason Olga put the racks in the rooms in the first place was because the closets were already full. In trying to provide a storage solution, she inadvertently set up the potential for mess because of mess.

You too may find examples of this throughout your house, particularly with regard to wicker baskets and cute containers. How many of those have you pulled into service because the proper storage space for various items was already full?

Be sure to check for Barnacles, Tinies, and Mess Because of Mess throughout your home and document them in your notebook.

My Most Embarrassing Messy House Story

—Cereal Killer—

BY MARTI T.

The kitchen counter was cluttered with dirty dishes, the evening newspaper, and a pile of mail as I hurriedly prepared the evening meal. We were expecting company so, as was generally the case with me, I went into frantic mode. Grabbing an empty Wheaties box, I swept a mound of potato peelings, carrot shavings, and the skin from a couple of large onions into the carton and set the box aside, thinking to toss it into the trash later. However, in my haste to straighten up the clutter, I forgot about the garbage in the box and quickly put the Wheaties box back where it belonged—on a shelf in the cupboard.

A full week later I was in the living room thumbing through a magazine when my husband went for a nightly snack—a bowl of cereal. Unfortunately, he was in the mood for Wheaties, so he poured himself a big bowl of...a putrid, rotting mess.

He never lets me hear the end of it.

Step 7

Consider the Clutter

Sell your possessions and give to the poor.
Provide purses for yourselves that will not wear out,
a treasure in heaven that will not be exhausted,
where no thief comes near and no moth destroys.
For where your treasure is, there your heart will be also.

LUKE 12:33-34

One of the most important observations I hope you make from all this scrutiny is that *you may have too much stuff.* I could be wrong, but chances are that the main reason your house is too hard to keep clean is because there are too many items in the house.

In a later chapter I'll help you purge that clutter, but for now it's simply important to understand the reasons it's there in the first place. According to the experts, there's a wide variety of reasons why we hang on to too many items. Some of the most common excuses are:

- you may need it someday
- you have sentimental attachment to it
- it was given to you as a gift
- you inherited it
- you got a really good deal on it

- you never thought about the fact that you already have one (or two or three)
- it holds the promise of fun or adventure
- you might be able to make something out of it
- you can get more for it if you hang on to it until you have time to sell it on eBay
- your children might want it someday
- somebody might need it

Too much of a good thing is still too much. Start looking at your home with a more discerning eye. Remember how it looked from atop your step stool! A home filled with unnecessary items can never be a house that cleans itself. How can it be if there's simply too much there to contain?

Right now, before you do another thing, turn to a fresh page in your notebook and write down what you are going to do with the clutter you will soon be weeding out of your home. Then gather the specific information you need to make that happen. If you're going to donate your unwanted stuff to a thrift store or charity or sell it through consignment, call to find out if they do house pick-ups and what you're supposed to do when you're ready to schedule one. If they don't do pick-ups, ask what the rules and times are for taking your stuff to them. Ask also what items they do and do not accept, and if they have any special rules, particularly with regard to how you package everything. You may end up donating to several charities, especially if there are items that some places will take and others won't. Keep the telephone numbers and information in your notebook so when you're ready with your stuff you can get it out of your house right away. Decide too on a temporary (*very* temporary) place to store the clutter you have decided to purge. For the loads you have to deliver yourself, consider using the trunk of your car for a temporary storage space. Every time your trunk gets full, make a run to the donation site.

If you're going to have a garage sale, clear some space now in an out-of-the-way area such as a shed or the back of your garage to put the items as they accumulate. Gather cardboard boxes or big garbage bags to put everything in. Consider keeping prepackaged price stickers with you as you declutter and stick them on each item as you go.

If you find this slows down your decluttering, don't do it. On the other hand, if putting a price sticker on something makes it easier for you to part with it, go for it. The goal is to do whatever it takes to pry this stuff out of your fingers for good. Start planning for your sale now, before the job of decluttering begins. Make sure too that you give yourself two important boundaries: 1) a time limit to hold that garage sale, beyond which the stuff gets donated, and 2) a promise that whatever doesn't sell on that day goes to charity that day or goes directly into the trash that day.

As you clear away clutter, if you end up having trouble letting things go, look for a further motivation. When I was doing my big decluttering, the Lord gave me a very special incentive: Just as I was starting to work my way through the kitchen and weed out all those extra pots and pans and dishes and small appliances that I rarely used, I learned through my church of a woman on a limited income who was going to be moving into her own apartment after years of living with her daughter. She had nothing for her new kitchen and no resources with which to buy anything. I arranged for all of my excess to go to her. As I went through my things and eliminated clutter, I found the job much easier and more rewarding because I knew there was someone specific who would benefit from every single thing I tossed. It was fun!

When you start to declutter, if you're having trouble lettings things go, ask God to make the recipients of your donations more tangible to you. Is there a battered women's shelter in your town? Call and see if some of their residents could use some clothes or toys or household items. You might also contact the leader of a local Celebrate Recovery or other addiction support group and see if any of the members are starting over and could use stuff to set up their households. When the time comes, even if the shelter or group passes the items along for you and you never have a chance to meet the people who are going to benefit from them, at least you'll know the items ended up in the hands of people who truly need them.

Finally, if you just can't seem to let enough of your stuff go, use what I call the "Maybe System." Put everything you know you *ought* to get rid of but just can't into cardboard boxes labeled "MAYBE." Then stash the boxes somewhere out of the way, such as in the attic. On your calendar, pick a date in six months (or even a year if that feels safer to you) and make a note to "Get Maybe boxes out of attic." When that date rolls around, it's final decision time. Hopefully during that passage of time you've seen that you don't need what's in the boxes and having a House That Cleans Itself is so wonderful you're not willing to let old clutter come back in. If that's the case, don't even peek inside the boxes. Send them on their way.

Using the Photos

There are three reasons that *Step 6* includes taking photos of your mess. The first and most important reason is the one you've already seen: Making and studying the pictures can help you better see and analyze the evidence that's in front of you.

The second reason the House That Cleans Itself (HTCI) System involves taking photos is so that you can have a photo record of your progress. Like having "before" and "after" pictures when you've been on a diet, sometimes it helps to look back to see how far you've come.

The day I began my own HTCI conversion in earnest, my home was in an especially bad state from one end to the other. Before I began, I bravely took out my camera and started snapping pictures. I still have those photos, and occasionally I'll look at them to remember where I was and how far I've come. Oddly enough, I treasure those pictures now because they are proof positive that the HTCI System works.

Nowadays, even in those occasional periods of prolonged neglect (due to book deadlines or extended travel or simply too many "to dos" in life converging at once), I'm amazed to see that when I return my attention to the house, it may need a good vacuuming or mopping, but the *disaster* isn't there anymore. The floors are clear; the kitchen is fine. At those times, I feel like the successful designer of a fireproof safe after a fire or a levee builder after the storm. The safe is intact! The levee held strong! The system works.

Preventing "Overwhelm"

The final reason I wanted you to take photos of your house was to help you frame the scope of your problem and keep it from overwhelming you. When you think of your entire house and the clutter purge that you are facing, the job ahead of you can feel enormous. But when you think in terms of each separate area that is contained in a photo, the task is not so daunting. You may not think you have the time or energy to weed out the unneeded stuff from an entire house, but you can handle everything that is shown in a picture of one space, right?

This "sense of overwhelm" was Beatrice's biggest problem with regard to clutter. She lived alone in a house that held 2500 square feet of stuff, a lifetime of accumulation she decided she needed to go through and clear out. Just thinking about processing room after room of possessions was so exhausting she was too discouraged to even give it a try.

Maybe some folks can't see the forest for the trees, but poor Beatrice couldn't see the trees for the forest. Taking photos of her entire house helped her focus on the smaller zones that needed attention. As long as she tackled her stuff *one photo's worth at a time,* she was able to keep going without wanting to give up. Eventually she made her way through her entire house. She kept more items than I would have (Beatrice has yet to deal with her psychological need to hoard), but she still managed to send five minivan loads of boxes and furniture to a local thrift store.

If the job ahead of you seems far too large to handle, I suggest you take this photo idea to the next level. Place prints of each of your pictures into their own photo album, in the order that you are going to work through your home. Using each picture as a guide, concentrate only on purging the area shown in that picture. If you did a thorough job of taking those pictures in the first place, when you reach the end of the photo album, you should be at the end of your house as well. Then you can sit back and enjoy the forest *and* the trees...not to mention the living room.

My Most Embarrassing Messy House Story

—Walk This Way—

BY KARLA P.

When I went away to college, my housekeeping went from bad to nonexistent. I shared a two-bedroom apartment with a friend, and though we kept the common areas fairly clean, my bedroom was always a disaster. Stuff was strewn everywhere, including on the floor.

One night we had a party and I kept the door to my bedroom closed. When I needed something from my room, I slipped inside, got what I needed by climbing over the mess, and came back out again without letting anyone see what was behind the door. Great strategy...or so I thought.

Unfortunately, what I didn't realize was that in my room, among the mess on the floor, was a new box of maxipads that had come open and spilled out. When I stepped on them, the adhesive was exposed on one and it had stuck to my shoe.

You've heard of people walking into a room with toilet paper on their shoe? Imagine walking into a party with a maxipad!

I've never been so embarrassed in my life.

Step 8

Comprehend You, Your Brain, and the Mess

Search me, O God, and know my heart; test me and know my anxious thoughts.

PSALM 139:23

Before you begin to put all of your steps into action, it's important to grasp certain essential truths about yourself and the way your brain works—and the problems those cause with regard to cleaning. Only when you understand the reasons behind your actions can you figure out ways to compensate for and work around those actions. If you happen to be married to a person who is more naturally neat than you are, he or she needs to read this chapter as well. After you've both read it, discuss the characteristics described here that apply to you. Sometimes simply understanding the cause of a behavior can ease much hurt, smoothing the way toward cooperation, teamwork, and lasting change.

Consider the following statements about some common characteristics of the housekeeping impaired.

Problem: You have a hard time remembering to pause, think, and do when it comes to the actions of daily life. Your brain is usually quite busy working on something unrelated to your body, so many of your physical actions are done without conscious thought. For example, when you're brushing your teeth, chances are you are also designing a living room, plotting a novel, or planting a garden—in your head, at least.

Because your brain is otherwise-occupied most of the time, any physical action that also requires a moment of thought (such as picking up a wayward sock, straightening a towel on a rack, or putting away a jacket rather than tossing it on a chair) is not going to get done. Your body may be there in the house, but your brain is not. You tend to ignore or not notice any action that requires you to interrupt your thought. This is how you are hard-wired. Are you a slob? Not at all. Unfortunately, to people who aren't this way, you can come across as messy and even inconsiderate.

Solution: How do you compensate for this type of impairment? In three ways:

1. *Set up your home so that doing the neat thing is as thoughtless a process as doing the messy thing.* For example, replace the chair you usually dump your jacket on with a standing coat rack.
2. *Force yourself to take a five-minute walk through your entire house once a day and focus on what's in front of you.* This is when you'll pick up those socks and straighten those towels. Set a timer if you have to, but on this walk do not do any heavy cleaning, just light straightening, and don't allow your mind to wander. As difficult as this is in the beginning, if you do it daily, it can become a fairly pain-free habit.
3. *Use labels everywhere so you don't have to think or remember when putting things away.* My family rolls their eyes at my labeled life that extends from the linen closet shelves to almost every shelf and bin in my office. But they don't have this out-of-sight, out-of-mind problem, so they don't understand that if I don't have labels to follow, I lose an enormous amount of time standing in front of a closet trying to bring my brain back into the moment,

consciously realize what I'm holding in my hand, and then remember where I previously decided that item ought to go. Without labels, cleaning is so much trouble that I'm less likely to do it.

Problem: If you can't see it, you don't remember it. As it relates to clutter, this is a far bigger problem than most people realize. Do you tend to forget about something if it's not out and visible to you? Could that be one reason your house is a mess? Because subconsciously you know if you put these things away you might never again find or even remember you have them? Maybe you don't have this problem so much with objects but you do with papers. If your desk is covered with horizontal piles, I daresay this is an issue for you. Let a piece of paper go (or, worse, place it in a vertical file folder), and you know for a fact you will forget it ever existed.

Solution: If you are a "can't remember it if you can't see it" person, your main household goal must always be to set up systems that aren't just useful but are also visible. Think see-through: clear bins, clear containers, clear drawers. Once I committed to using only clear storage, it made a world of difference! One money-saving tip: Buy clear storage containers at after-Christmas sales. Though clear usually costs more than opaque the rest of the year, the ones with clear bottoms and red and green lids (for storing decorations) are very reasonable when they're on sale.

You also need to set up whatever memory-jogging helps you can throughout your house, such as bulletin boards, big signs, labels, and reminders. Be sure to integrate them into your décor in such a way that they can easily be hidden or camouflaged when you want to tidy up.

Finally, you may need to forego vertical files almost entirely and find some other substitute for your papers. It's not easy to live a file-free life, but you can carry this idea much further than you might think by substituting horizontal sorters, boxes, and drawers.

Problem: When you organize, you tend to overdo by creating too many categories. Too many subdivisions makes sorting complicated and challenging. Even if you set up a good, simple sorting system by following someone else's guidelines, when it comes time to use it, you may find yourself simply standing there in confusion, item in hand, wondering what category that item is most closely related to. And even if you do manage to give it a home, later you can't remember which category you chose, forcing you to dig through all applicable file folders to find the missing paper.

If you don't know whether the receipt for your window unit air conditioner should be filed under major purchase receipts (it *was* $250), tax records (I *am* using it in my home office), appliances (technically, is an air conditioner an appliance?), then this is an issue for you.

Solution: To best deal with it, think in terms "broader is better." Use boxes or drawers rather than files, and give them more general categories (for example, that air conditioner receipt could go into a box more broadly labeled "Papers related to stuff I own"). This system may look inefficient to others, but for you this might be the answer to a lifetime of struggling with your tendency to overanalyze.

As for your tendency to overorganize, whenever you set up any new system, from your spice cabinet to your CD collection, always pause and ask yourself if you're carrying it too far. Then ask someone else! His or her input will help you see if your organization is too extensive, causing more problems than it will solve.

Problem: When you clean, you tend to get lost in the process, which costs you so much time that you aren't able to finish the job. It is a strange phenomenon that most people who consider themselves housekeeping impaired will flip to the opposite side of the spectrum once they get rolling. Before they know it, they're alphabetizing the entire CD collection or are on their hands and knees with a razor blade, scraping away gunk from along the base of the back door.

This is another big problem for me. I can't even remember how many times I set out to clean the "whole house, top to bottom" and never made it past the second room. If you have trouble judging time—both estimating how much time something is going to take and how much time is passing when you're actually doing it—then that compounds the problem.

Solution: I have three ideas for you:

1. *Always look at the "big picture."* Take a quick inventory of a room first and force yourself to begin with the most important areas. For instance, in the kitchen, if there are dirty dishes in the sink and newspapers spread across the table, don't start by washing the windows.
2. *Clean with a portable timer.* Divide the number of minutes you have to spend by the number of areas you want to clean. The resulting number is how long to set the timer for each room. When the timer goes off, whether you are finished in there or not, move to the next room. Start the timer again. As long as you cooperate with the timer, this technique will keep you moving throughout the house.
3. *Clean with others.* Trade off with a friend. You give her two hours every Tuesday, she gives you two every Thursday. Or try what I call the *Room-to-Room Sequencing* method, described fully in the section "How to Clean a House That Cleans Itself," in Part 3 of this book. When I'm sequence cleaning, I know I have to stay on task because there are two people waiting for me to finish so they can get in there and do their jobs.

Problem: You are a perfectionist, or similarly, you are an all-or-nothing cleaner. You're not going to clean at all unless you can do it right and/or do it completely. The problem is that life doesn't often allow the luxury of that much uninterrupted time.

My mother tells the story of when she was newly married and eager to win a coveted "Good Housekeeping" certificate given once a year by the management of the apartment complex where she and my dad lived. On the day the contest judge arrived to inspect their apartment, it was spotlessly clean and not one thing was out of place. The judge was impressed, and it looked like my mother was going to get the certificate she worked so hard for...until the judge grabbed the edge of the gas stovetop and lifted the top to reveal a greasy mess. (Never having had a gas stove and because the hinges were hidden, my mother didn't know the lid would lift or that grime would settle there.) Despite all her hard work, she didn't qualify for the certificate.

The perfectionistic bent in Mom couldn't make her home perfect even though she did her best. She just didn't know everything...and, really, who does?

When I think of this story, I'm so glad it's not the 1950s anymore! I can't imagine someone coming into my home and judging my efforts. Even at its cleanest, my house would not win any prizes. Fighting this tendency toward perfectionism myself, I have spent a lot of time in the last few years changing my standards for what clean really looks like, which in the strange mathematics of perfectionism has actually resulted in a much cleaner house.

Are your standards so skewed that you would sacrifice *average daily cleanliness* for *perfect occasional cleanliness?* This all-or-nothing approach simply doesn't work in the day-to-day reality of life. Just as you can't lose weight if you eat like a king for six days and then fast on the seventh, you can't conquer your mess if you avoid all cleaning for six days and then go crazy cleaning from one end of your house to the other on the seventh.

Solution: To combat this problem, you have to see that it *is* a problem and not just a personality quirk. Perfectionists and all-or-nothingers can absolutely *paralyze* themselves, preferring complete inaction to doing something imperfectly or incompletely. Consequently, they miss out on a lot of life because they avoid having people come to their homes except when their places are perfectly clean. If this sounds like you, I don't have any work-around tips to help you compensate. This one must be attacked head-on by refusing to allow these tendencies to have an effect on your cleaning behavior.

When I first realized this for myself, I had not yet converted my home to a House That Cleans Itself, so there was no consistency regarding the state of cleanliness. On any given day, the house might appear sparkling and spotless, dirty and disastrous, or somewhere in-between. When I saw that my perfectionist tendencies were contributing to this problem, I resolved to change. That change began with *raising my lowest standards* and *lowering my highest standards,* hoping they would more often *meet in the middle.* I also decided to stop going nuts trying to make the house perfect every time company was coming. This was hard for me, especially in the beginning, but I forced myself to have people over on a regular basis whether the house was spotlessly clean that day or not. A house that cleans itself is one that's *clean enough.* If you are housekeeping-impaired, aiming for more than that is a sure recipe for disaster.

To help conquer my perfectionism, I came up with a saying: "They're not here to see a clean house, they're here to see us." I told myself this when friends stopped by for a quick hello and the breakfast dishes weren't in the dishwasher yet. I told myself this when my dad visited and we had to clear some boxes out the spare bedroom to give him somewhere to sleep. But slowly, as I worked to conquer those tendencies, the strangest shift began to occur. Once the house didn't have to be perfect sometimes, it began to be okay more of the time. The cleanest days weren't so clean, true, but the messy days weren't so messy either.

The day I knew I had sufficiently conquered my perfectionism was the day I gave my daughters a surprise party. I invited all of the guests to hide in the dining room even though I had run out of time before the party and hadn't been able to clear the table of several stacks of papers or vacuum the floor. (After the moment of surprise, the party was going to be relocated to the back deck, which had received pre-party attention and was clean and nicely decorated.) Despite the fact that there were 15 people crammed together in that less-than-perfect dining room, I realized they really weren't there to see a clean house. They were there for us, to celebrate with my older daughter, who was graduating from the eighth grade, and to celebrate with my younger daughter, who had just the week before been baptized. Crouching on the rug that had some crumbs on it, listening to my husband usher the unsuspecting kids into the house, holding my breath in that final second before we all jumped up and yelled "Surprise!" I realized how far I had come. The way my house looked was no longer more important than the people who gathered in it.

This should be the goal of every perfectionist: to *not* need to be perfect. This should be the goal of every all-or-nothinger: to *not* have to finish everything. Ask God to begin to work such a change in you.

Problem: Through past problems and failures, you have developed aversions to many conventional tools and methods of organizing, such as putting papers into file folders. If you've spent a lifetime feeling stupid or guilty because conventional tools and methods don't work for you, it's time to stop beating yourself up.

Solution: Throw convention to the wind and base your solutions on the tools and methods that *do* work for you. Give yourself the opportunity to try new solutions. Think outside the box! For example, I don't know why sliding papers into a slot doesn't appeal to me but dropping them into an open bin does. I have given up trying to figure out the "why" and instead decided to focus on the "what": what works for me in keeping this house clean, in helping me organize, in guiding me through the hours I am given in a day.

Ditch the "oughts," as in "you ought" to do something this way or that way. Says who? Do it in whatever way works for you. Just don't give up on finding ways to make it work.

Problem: In reaction to failed conventional methods, you feverishly acquire unconventional or complicated organizational devices, thinking they will finally solve all of your problems. Some unconventional devices can be very helpful, but many "organizational" tools actually suck up your time and in the end make more of a mess.

When conventional *and* unconventional tools fail, rather than racing around to find yet another tool, use what you've learned about yourself and your issues to come up with a better, simpler way of doing things.

Terri thought she had finally found the perfect tool for handling, sorting, and using coupons. She mounted a "coupon handler bulletin board" in her laundry room that was divided vertically by category and horizontally by expiration date. For about a month she diligently placed her coupons in their appropriate squares, excited that she was finally going to take advantage of the great savings these coupons offered.

The problem was that whenever Terri went to the grocery store, she usually forgot to take the correct coupons. Even when she remembered them, once she got to the checkout line, she was so distracted with unloading, bagging, and paying that she would forget to pull them out of her purse and use them. Her enthusiasm dimmed, and at home she grew less diligent about sorting the coupons. Eventually she had a half-filled fancy bulletin board and four boxes of coupons to sort, most of which she was more than likely never going to use. Terri was frustrated.

Solution: Rather than beat herself up about it, I told her to think about the lessons she'd learned from the failure of her system. Her conclusion: She needed to give up the idea of using coupons entirely. For people with "out of sight, out of mind" issues, coupons cause more trouble than they're worth. She tossed out the coupons *and* the bulletin board and never let herself feel guilty about all those "lost savings" again. Instead, she focused on other ways to cut costs, such as joining a warehouse club and buying her veggies at a local produce stand.

When conventional *and* unconventional tools fail, rather than racing around to find yet another tool, use what you've learned about yourself and your issues to come up with a better, simpler way of doing things. It's not about the tools; it's about your behavior and your brain. It's about figuring out what you *can* do to make cleaning and organizing feel less like a desperate swim upstream and more like a lazy paddle down the river.

Ditch This Ought

"I ought to clip and use coupons."

Says who?

Don't do it if it doesn't work for you!

Problem: When you decide to change, you jump in too far, too fast, and too enthusiastically...and burn out before you're done. Over the years the people who know me best have learned not to invest too heavily in some of my enthusiasms because they know most of them will peter out long before I establish true change or reach the end of a project. Is this true for you as well?

This is more than a personality issue. At its core, it's a spiritual issue. When we go running too quickly down a primrose path at full steam, we're running ahead of God—ahead of his timing and ahead of his blessing. Psalm 25:4-5 says, "Show me your ways, O LORD, teach me your paths; guide me in your truth and teach me, for you are God my Savior, and my hope is in you all day long." In our hurry we leave no room for learning or guidance. Our hope is not in God but in our own ideas and excitement. Psalm 46:10 says, "Be still, and know that I am God." How hard it is for some of us to be still! But that's exactly the character trait God yearns to develop in us.

Solution: Resist the urge to run off half-cocked every time you think you've found a new and better way to conquer mess. If God is in what you want to do, he will reveal that to you in his time. Resolve to stop entering into household purges and changes—even the one described in this book—without first fully grasping the scope of what lies ahead. Whether you end up using the House That Cleans Itself

System or something else entirely, make a commitment this time and stick with it to the very end.

Isaiah 40:29 reminds us that "[God] gives strength to the weary and increases the power of the weak." Rather than giving up when you grow weary, as you've done in the past, this time claim his promise that "those who hope in the LORD will renew their strength. They will soar on wings like eagles; they will run and not grow weary, they will walk and not be faint" (Isaiah 40:31). If you do find yourself feeling frustrated or exhausted, relax, go slower, or take a break by choosing a smaller task you can conquer quickly. Then go back to your original endeavor.

Yes, it may take longer than you wish to purge your home of a lifetime of accumulations. Yes, it may get boring and frustrating sometimes to convert your house to a House That Cleans Itself. Yes, you may get tired. But no, you can't use your tiredness as an excuse to stop fixing this broken part of your life. When you reach the end of yourself, allow your weariness and loss of enthusiasm to send you straight into the arms of the one who wants to renew you. Be still. Listen to him. Worship him. Honor him.

Then get back at it. Know this for sure: Eagles' wings are the very best housekeeping tool you'll ever find.

My Most Embarrassing Messy House Story

—A Better Mouse Trap—

BY JESSIE R.

Living in a farmhouse, we have mice. Lots of them. Even though our cat is an excellent mouser, she still misses a few here and there. One of them set up shop in the oven. I decided to try the new mousetraps, which are basically a tray of adhesive. Because I suspected the mouse had invited friends, I got the rat-sized one. I caught a couple in the first trap. Giddy with success, I put a second one in the oven.

Unfortunately, I later forgot about it and turned the oven on to preheat. The adhesive bubbled over, the tray melted, the house filled with fumes, the smoke detector wouldn't quit, and we had to open all the doors and windows and have a picnic supper that night. When the oven cooled off I had to scrape the adhesive off the bottom with a putty knife.

At least the trap had been empty when I did it. I shudder to think what it would have been like to clean up all that mess—and roasted mouse too.

Step 9

Estimate, Commit, Plan

The end of a matter is better than its beginning, and patience is better than pride.

ECCLESIASTES 7:8

Just how bad off is your house really? I ask because it's time for some honesty. Take a wide-eyed appraisal of how cluttered your home really is, how many of your systems don't work, and how quickly your home falls apart once it's clean. There is a very wide spectrum between a place that's marginally messy and needs a little help and one that's a giant disaster zone from one end to the other. The problem is that people who are housekeeping impaired are also often *time* impaired. Unable to calculate the true time that most tasks will take, they jump in fast and work hard, but then they lose hope when they begin to understand the scope of what's really involved. To prevent that from happening this time, it's important to calculate the job of making your home a house that cleans itself.

First let's do a quick evaluation. On a scale of one to ten, with ten being the highest and one being the lowest, circle the number you feel best represents the truth.

1. *Your natural ability as a cleaner*

   1 2 3 4 5 6 7 8 9 10

   To calculate this consider these questions.

- Were you tidy or sloppy as a child?
- Do you notice mess or tend to see past it?
- What happens to your environment when you're busy or not really paying attention? Does it remain clean, fall apart, or stay the same?
- What emotions do you associate with housecleaning? Are they positive, negative, or neutral?
- Has anyone ever told you that your household systems seem illogical?
- Do you make cleaning harder for yourself by how you've organized your time or possessions?
- Are you ever embarrassed by the state of your car, inside or out?
- Do you wonder why other people sail through life's tasks while you struggle with them?

2. *Your knowledge of housekeeping*

   1 2 3 4 5 6 7 8 9 10

   To calculate this ask yourself these questions.

   - On average, how clean was your home when you were growing up?
   - Were you taught how to clean by instruction?
   - Were you taught how to clean by example?
   - Do you know how often various cleaning tasks should be performed?
   - Are you aware of the obscure jobs that are necessary only once or twice a year?

3. *The cleanliness of your home most of the time*

   1 2 3 4 5 6 7 8 9 10

   To calculate this one ask yourself these questions.

- How clean is your house right now?
- If unexpected guests showed up, how comfortable would you be with the cleanliness of your home?
- If you learned at the last minute someone was coming over, how many rooms would you let them see?
- Have you perfected the art of the last-minute fix-up—tossing dirty dishes in the oven, toys in the dryer, and everything else behind the couch?
- How would your spouse and children score this one? Is your home satisfactorily clean to everyone who lives there except you?
- How many days of each month (or hours of each day) would you say your house has gotten out of control and needs to be cleaned?

Now add up those three figures, for a possible total of 30.

Your score: _____

Scoring

21 or higher: You're probably reading this book to pick up a few new tips or to figure out how to help a less-capable friend or relative. If you got a perfect 30, perhaps you need to reevaluate your standards—or at the very least open your own cleaning service and cash in on your astonishing ability to handle dirt and clutter.

11 to 20: You're in good company; most people's scores fall in this range. You have some natural ability and some knowledge. Your home is satisfactorily clean at least some of the time. As you work through this book, keep an open mind about how you can make a good thing even better.

10 or less: You've probably spent a lifetime struggling with mess, guilt, and low self-esteem regarding your cleaning abilities. I know firsthand how demoralizing a messy house can be, especially when you've given it your all and the mess persists. Don't give up hope, and don't give up on yourself! The House That Cleans Itself System will be a tremendous help to you!

Estimating Cleaning Time

Now that you've figured out your housekeeping score, here is a very general timetable based on working at your house conversion consistently:

21 or higher: Converting your home to the House That Cleans Itself System could take anywhere from one week to a month.

11 to 20: Converting your home to the HTCI System could take anywhere from a few weeks to a few months.

10 or less: Converting your home to the HTCI System could take six months or more. But don't despair! Your home didn't get that way overnight, and it's not going to be fixed that quickly either. Just be diligent, and in the end your efforts will be rewarded tenfold.

Remember, these are just estimations. Your actual conversion to a House That Cleans Itself may take less or more time. I've included these estimates because I want you to enter into the process with a full understanding of your commitment. The HTCI System is not a quick fix or an overnight solution. Unlike other plans you may have tried, however, it will be your *final* solution.

Commitment

Now that you understand the time involved, are you ready to commit? Converting your home to a house that cleans itself may make your mess *seem* worse in the beginning, but hang in there.

You'll need dedication and enthusiasm. I encourage you to take it on. You won't regret it!

Plan

If you need extra motivation to stay on track, why not plan now to host a future event? Take out your calendar, add a month's buffer to the "convert to a HTCI time estimation," and choose a date to host a gathering in your home. Whether you plan to have a dinner party, a brunch, or a family reunion, pick the date and start spreading the word now.

I learned this trick years ago when my husband and I hosted Thanksgiving for his family. As we worked hard to get the house company-ready for more than 20 relatives, I realized how many extra household tasks we were getting done because of that motivation. My husband worked even harder than I did, tackling those "honey do" items I'd been asking him about all year. Once we were in the countdown to Thanksgiving, he really buckled down and accomplished everything on his list.

Nowadays, we offer to host Thanksgiving almost every year because we enjoy his family and our time together *and* because we know it encourages us to get our bigger house projects completed. My suggestion is that you schedule a similar annual event in your home to keep you moving along when you might be tempted to let things slide.

One caveat: Only you know if setting an impending commitment will give you extra energy and motivation or add unwanted, unneeded stress. If the thought of assigning a finish date to your conversion and putting out the word about a post-conversion gathering at your house makes you feel stressed or pressured in a bad way, don't do it! The last thing you want to do is stress yourself out. The only pressure we want in this process is good, helpful pressure.

The 10 Principles of the HTCI System

Through research, trial and error, and countless interviews with people who struggle in the area of housekeeping, I've developed 10 principles that serve as the foundation for the HTCI System:

1. *Change the house to fit the behavior.* The more your house can be changed to accommodate and support your family's behaviors, the more it will stay clean.
2. *Change the behavior to fit the house, but only after you've changed the house as much as possible.* Because not every issue can be solved by changing the house, there will be times when you need to adapt the house *and* change the behavior.
3. *Control your "expected messy areas" and "sight zones."* Design clever ways to conceal those areas in your home that might appear cluttered to an outsider, but in truth the areas are merely functional, such as the family bulletin board or the front door launching pad. In a later chapter, you'll also learn about using sight zones to make your house appear even cleaner.
4. *Think like a hotel.* Because so much of a hotel's operating costs are for housekeeping labor, the industry has streamlined the cleaning process as much as possible. Choices in carpets, lighting fixtures, bedspreads, and so forth are made with an eye toward the guests' comfort and for ease of cleaning. The placement of the beds (three sides accessible for ease in changing linens), the choice of linens and towels (monochromatic for ease in laundering and stain removal), and even the maid carts (everything needed for cleaning is rolled from room to room) are set up to make life easier. Walls are usually papered rather than painted (no fingerprints show), televisions are hidden behind closed doors, and coffee machines and accessories are gathered together on one tray. Hotels also frequently use the "up and away" principle, where

everything possible is mounted on the wall rather than sitting on a horizontal surface.

Though you don't want to live in a sterile environment, think how much easier it is to clean and dust when there's nothing to move out of the way and put back.

5. *Think like a housecleaning service.* When it comes to cleaning, remaining detached and businesslike will keep your housecleaning in proper perspective. A home should be a haven, a blessing, and a privilege, yes, but it's not a representation of your value as a human being. It also isn't a living object that has thoughts or feelings. A house is an inanimate object, a tool for living, and a shelter.
6. *Emphasize simplicity.* This principle applies in three ways:
   - *Less stuff equals less mess,* so purge the clutter!
   - *Simple choices equal simple cleaning,* so avoid ornate, highly detailed furnishings and other possessions whenever possible.
   - *Keep it uniform to keep it clean.* The fewer surfaces and finishes in your home, the fewer cleaning products and processes will be required to keep it clean.
7. *Engineer convenience.* Like a martial arts master who uses a person's own weight and force to propel him toward the mat, use your family's natural tendency toward convenience to keep your house clean.
8. *Utilize the power of beauty.* The more aesthetically pleasing a room is, the more likely it is to remain clean.
9. *Camouflage wherever possible.* From permanent characteristics such as linoleum patterns or carpet colors to more temporary items such as bedding choices and appliance finishes, resolve to make an item's ability to camouflage dirt and stains a priority when making decisions about what to put into your home.

10. *Do everything with an eye toward maintenance.* No matter how successful you are at getting your home to look great, if you can't maintain that look day after day, you're in a never-ending battle. By making follow-through a built-in part of the plan, you guarantee your success.

My Most Embarrassing Messy House Story

—Busted?—

BY ALICIA R.

At the time this happened, I'd just had my third baby in five years and was faithfully helping my husband milk the cows every day. Needless to say, with a newborn and two toddlers and a farm, things got a little shaggy. One day two nice young men with clipboards and ID badges showed up and knocked on the door.

"Good morning, ma'am," one of them said. "We're from the Health Department."

All I could think was, *Who told you about the house?*

Apparently noticing my expression, the other one added hurriedly, "It's O.K. We're doing a well-water survey!"

Step 10

Create a Devotional Area

Fix these words of mine in your hearts and minds; tie them as symbols on your hands and bind them on your foreheads. Teach them to your children, talking about them when you sit at home and when you walk along the road, when you lie down and when you get up.

DEUTERONOMY 11:18-19

For this final step of preparation, you're going to set up a place to have daily devotion time. (If you already have a good, daily devotional routine, make sure that the area is clean and peaceful. Then move on to the next chapter. If you don't have a devotional area or routine, complete this step before proceeding with your HTCI conversion.) Daily devotion time with God is important. If you continue with the HTCI conversion without first establishing this routine, you'll get so caught up in housecleaning (yes, this may happen!) that you might let your quiet time fall to the wayside. But going to God on a daily basis and keeping him at the center of your heart and home is the key to lasting change. So commit to having this special time and place with God.

First, what time of day—every day—will you be able to grab some alone time with God? It doesn't have to be extensive. If you are the mother of small children and can squeeze in only five minutes, commit to God those five minutes. He knows your heart and your situation.

Once you know the time of day you'll do your devotions, you will have a better idea of a suitable place. For example:

- If you're going to get up early, you might not want to do it in a room that takes a while to get warm.
- If you're going to do it while others are sleeping, you won't want to be where you might disturb them with your reading light or rustling pages.
- If you're going to do it while people are in the house, you'll want to choose an area with a door that closes.

Ideally you should find (or set up) a comfy chair beside a good reading light. Just make sure the chair isn't so comfy you'll fall asleep! Now gather the following supplies:

- *A Bible.* I love my Ryrie Study Bible in the NIV translation. Use whatever translation and format you like best.
- *A Bible highlighter* if you like to mark important verses.
- *A pen or pencil and a blank notebook or prayer journal.* Your prayer journal can be as minimal or extensive as you want it to be, but at the very least it should include a brief list of the things and people you are praying about and God's answers. Update this regularly. Nothing reinforces our understanding of answered prayers better than a record of our requests and God's answers. At least once a year, maybe around New Year's Day or on your birthday, thumb through your prayer journal and marvel at God's faithfulness and ingenuity in answering your petitions.
- *A paper, chart, or book that shows your Bible reading schedule* if you are working through a program. Most everyone has seen typical read-the-Bible-in-a-year plans, but did you know there are also plans for reading the Bible over several years (for intensive, drawn-out study) and even for reading it in 90 days (for a fast, broad overview)?

Reading through the Bible in a variety of ways can help open your mind to new truths each time.

- *A few good devotional books.* I used to think I had to stick with one devotional book for an entire year, but then I realized that I could keep several devotional books at hand and switch back and forth between them at will. Some days I skip the devotional book entirely and just focus on a Bible passage instead. Most days, though, I like the structure that a devotional book gives, and I choose which one I want to read based on how clear my brain feels, how deep I want to go, or where I need help. Consequently, I make sure to keep on hand one that offers complex and profound truths, one that's relevant to my day-to-day life, and one that's light and easy for a quick read.
- *Any "comfort" items that will help to put you in a worshipful frame of mind.* Some people worship best in a setting that is austere, such as the cold stone of a monastery or in a small prayer closet. But you may be more likely to immerse yourself in the process and stay with it longer if you take a few steps to make your devotional area comfortable. God just wants you to come to him—however you come to him! Thus, you might include a lap blanket, a candle and matches, a small CD player with a praise music CD waiting inside, a box of tissues, a shawl, and a pillow on the floor for when you feel called to kneel. The point is to have a place that's ready and waiting for your devotional time at a moment's notice.
- *A cheap kitchen timer.* Yes, you need a timer if you: 1) avoid daily devotions because you know you'll get lost in them and end up spending extra time you don't have to spare, or 2) cannot truly focus on daily devotions because you are too distracted watching the clock so you'll know when to stop. Whenever possible, don't put God on a schedule, or keep a tight lid on your worship time, or ignore the

tuggings of the Holy Spirit if more prayer is needed. But if you avoid devotions because you are afraid of the time commitment, setting a timer will free you to meet with God much more often.

Whatever you choose to include in your devotion area, the goal is to set up a permanent grouping of items that do not get carried anywhere else for any other purpose.

Setting Up Your Space

Once you have chosen the space where you plan to do your devotions and have gathered the necessary items, you need to choose where the items will go. The best choice for now is to put everything in a tote bag or basket (or a box that locks if you want to keep your journal private). Place it within easy reach of where you'll be sitting. These items are going to be shifted around when you sweep through that room on your House That Cleans Itself attack, so the points right now are for them to be *accessible to the place where you will use them* and *together in one container or holder.*

These items will be assigned a more permanent location as you work through the House That Cleans Itself System.

Building the Habit

Tomorrow, at the time you have decided upon, go to this place and spend at least five minutes doing your devotions. No matter how busy you are, there must be five spare minutes somewhere in your day for you to read a Bible passage and pray. The next day, try for a little longer, say ten minutes. Slowly work your way up in time each day, if you can, but always allow yourself the freedom to spend only five minutes if that's all you have. In the past, chances are it would have taken twice as long as that just to find your Bible and gather the items you need.

How much time should you work up to? That depends on your other obligations and even your attention span, but for most people daily devotions last anywhere from five minutes to an hour, with the average being 15 to 30 minutes. During that time you can read the allotted Bible verses, read that day's page in a devotional book, write or list in your prayer journal, and pray.

Remember, coming to God this way is a privilege and a joy! Yes, it takes a certain amount of commitment to get rolling on this as a daily habit, but if after several weeks you find that you are still doing it only out of obligation or duty, something is wrong. Speak to your pastor or a wise Christian friend to help you figure out what might be hindering your time with God. Consider also that often when prayer time does not flow and feels more like a burden than an opportunity, it may be because there is some unconfessed sin that's coming between you and God.

Finally, take time each day to read and pray, but also remember to quietly meditate and listen for God's leading. A messy house can be a noisy house spiritually speaking, and the more you turn down that noise and focus on God, the more you can hear his voice and understand his plan for you.

Getting Started

Don't forget: You have an appointment in this place, at the time you have determined, every day of the week, beginning tomorrow.

Be there. Consistently.

It will have a greater impact on you, your life, and your home than you can ever imagine.

Now that you are in a position to have daily private time with God in your home, it is time to move to the next phase in your home's conversion to a House That Cleans Itself.

Are you ready? It's time to CONVERT.

My Most Embarrassing Messy House Story

—A Telltale Ring—

BY L.W.

Early in my married life I struggled to keep up with three kids and all the housework. Some things had to go. Well, I knew I'd let it go too long when one of my children's friends looked at our bathtub in horror.

"Ewww!" the six-year-old pixie exclaimed as she pointed at the dark ring around the inside of the tub. "My mommy would never let me take a bath in there."

"Oh," my daughter answered, "that's just so we know how far to fill the water."

I slunk away, and from that day on, we never had a ring around our tub again.

Part 2

Get Set...

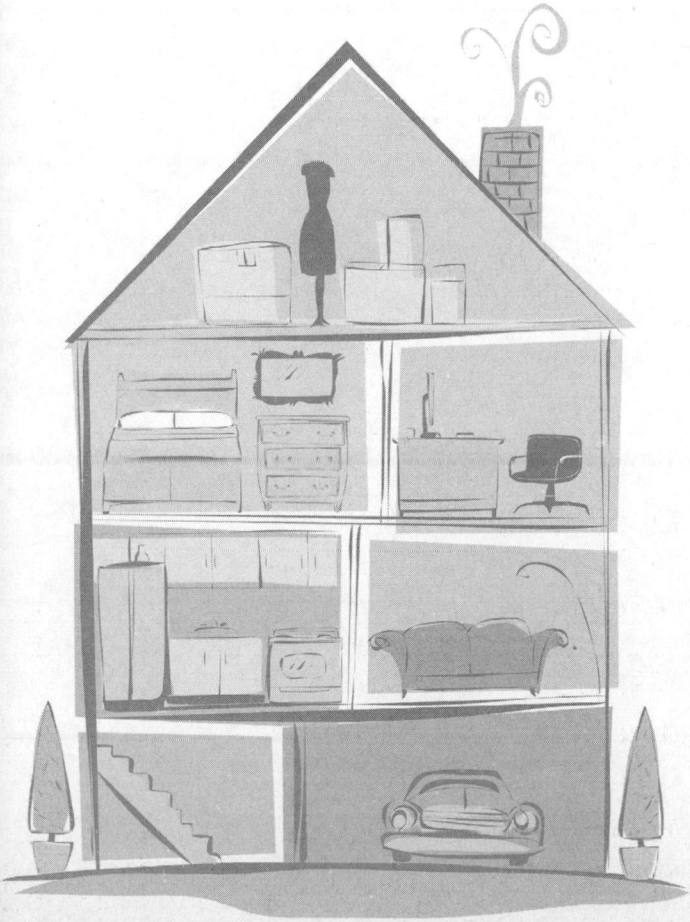

Introducing the CONVERT System

His eyes are on the ways of men;
he sees their every step.

JOB 34:21

Are you ready to dig in? Then gather up the following items and let's go!

- your notebook, with your Flow Plan drawn or stapled inside
- a pen or pencil
- a box of large black garbage bags
- a box of large white garbage bags
- two brand-new plastic trash cans without lids, preferably "tall kitchen" size or larger
- a laundry basket or large plastic bin with handles
- cardboard boxes with the lid flaps cut off, in a variety of sizes, for sorting
- more cardboard boxes (with lids intact) with MAYBE written on the sides
- a package of disposable plastic cups
- a permanent marker
- a labelmaker or some blank stickers

- a measuring tape
- a blanket or quilt
- cleaning supplies such as rags, all-purpose cleaner, glass cleaner, vacuum, bucket, mop

The HTCI process is straightforward, but you really need to think of your house as "under construction" since this is going to take a while. Starting with the area on your Flow Plan defined as #1, you're going to work your way through your entire house and property in numerical order, following your Floor Plan and working at a pace that is best for you.

Make sure not to spend so much time on any given day or for so many days in a row that you burn out before the job is complete. Remember the time estimation from *Step 9* and scale your expectations accordingly. Whether you can put in an hour a day twice a week or five hours a day six days a week, eventually you will make it to the end of this conversion. When you are done, you will be the proud and much-less-overburdened inhabitant of a House That Cleans Itself. Your efforts will have paid off, and you'll reap the benefits of less stress and more time.

CONVERT Each Area

In each area on your Flow Plan, you will be doing the following:

C lear out the clutter

O pen up and clean

N eaten, organize, and solve problem spots

V erify and set up Stations as needed

E xamine Sight Zones

R ecord future improvements needed

T ake steps now for ongoing maintenance

To have the fastest impact on your house, *complete all eight steps in one area before you start the next area.* This may not be the most efficient way to declutter or clean, but it is the best way to convert your home to a House That Cleans Itself for four reasons:

- Once an area is finished, it will stay neater and cleaner and require less time to maintain.
- You will learn as you go, seeing what really does work and what needs additional tweaking. This will help you do an even better job in subsequent areas.
- Changing from one task to the next helps you circumvent some of your natural housekeeping "impairments," such as difficulty in making decisions or focusing, by allowing you to do these things in short bursts rather than prolonged agony.
- The payoff of completion as you finish each area will spur you on. For a project this big, you need payoffs all along the way.

When you're finished each day, drape the blankets over the boxes and bags and proclaim that what's underneath is off limits for now. This will keep things looking as neat as possible and keep everyone from rummaging through the items to "save" them or move them.

My Most Embarrassing Messy House Story

—The Night Bandit—

BY TOMMY L.

Once when I was in my 20s, I came home from a date to find a surprise in my bedroom. Living on the third floor of an old apartment building in a fairly urban area, I had left the window open without a screen, never expecting a raccoon to climb inside and make himself at home on my desk.

I called the police, who came right away. Not knowing what else to do, they stood in the doorway of the bedroom and threw things at the animal until it finally got fed up and left, climbing out the way it had come in. We then closed the window behind it.

As the cops were leaving, I thanked them for their trouble. They said it was no problem, but that it was a shame I hadn't gotten home before the raccoon tore my whole bedroom apart.

Red-faced, I didn't have the nerve to tell them that the raccoon hadn't done a thing. The bedroom looked like that before the animal got there!

11

Clear Out the Clutter

(CONVERT)

There is a time for everything, and a season for every activity under heaven...a time to search and a time to give up, a time to keep and a time to throw away.

ECCLESIASTES 3:1,6

Many excellent books have been written on the subject of clearing clutter, so I won't fill pages and pages about it here. I do have a few points to make that will help as you face each of your areas and separate the wheat from the chaff.

Two Types of Clutterers

First, it's important to note that there are two types of clutterers: "clay" and "cement."

"Clay" clutterers (so named because they are pliable and can be molded) tend to hang on to stuff for a variety of reasons, but their cluttering problem springs more from habit, personality style, lack of knowledge, lack of discipline, or distractibility than it does from any real *need* to clutter. If clay clutterers will focus on fixing the reasons they clutter in the first place, they can be quite successful in changing their ways. Although pack rats by nature will always struggle somewhat, by setting up specific routines, habits, and strategies, clay clutterers can learn to live with this problem and keep it from getting the best of them.

"Cement" clutterers (so named because they are about as difficult to mold and change as, well, cement) also hang on to stuff for a variety of reasons, but at its core their cluttering problem springs from a deep-rooted need to keep things. Cement clutterers think of themselves as "pack rats," but in truth they may be suffering from a more serious condition known as "hoarding."

Hoarding is defined by the specific behaviors of acquiring too much and discarding too little (even items that most people would consider useless). Consequently, they create such clutter-filled living spaces that those spaces cannot be used for their intended purposes. It will be difficult for a hoarder to have a House That Cleans Itself until he deals with the issues behind his behavior. If you're a cement clutterer, explore what's going on. Don't be afraid to set out on the HTCI journey, just be sure to seek help for the hoarding issue first. In time, you *can* become a clay clutterer...and successfully complete this project!

How to Declutter

Whether you are made of clay or cement, if you are a clutterer, chances are you have spent a lifetime hearing different methods for clearing away your stuff. Most experts suggest asking yourself several key questions, such as "Do I really need this?" and "Have I used it in the last year?"

I say that if you were capable of asking and answering those sorts of questions, the clutter never would have built up in the first place. Do you really want to get rid of clutter? Then embrace this single truth:

> *Every possession you have, from the tiniest button to the biggest piece of furniture, takes with it a piece of your time.*

You spend time on your stuff when you acquire it, when you clean it, when you move it, when you shove it into a box and put it into the basement, when you kick it out of the way because you stepped on it, when you leave it out and the kids mess with it, when you get it dirty and have to wash it, when you fish it out from under the bed, when you hold it in your hand and try to decide what to do with it, when you sort it again, when you store it again, when you decorate with it, when you think about it, when you feel guilty about it, when you dust it, and so on. Think of something completely insubstantial in your home, such as a safety pin or an emery board. If you have ever interacted with that item at all, you have spent time on it merely because it is one of your possessions.

The questions to ask yourself are not value judgments about when you used it last or when you might need it again. To clutterers, there are too many shades of gray in those questions. Instead, face the black-and-white reality of the true trade-off you're making. When you are decluttering, with every single item you own ask yourself these questions:

- Is this item worth my time?
- Does what I get from this item provide a fair trade-off considering I have to clean it and store it?
- Do I want to spend another second in the future fooling with it or do I want to get rid of it now so it will no longer cost me a thing?

Probably both the safety pin and the emery board are worth keeping. When you pop a button at the last minute or have a broken nail, your time investment in those items pays off.

But what about that cute little wicker basket you've never quite figured out what to do with? What about that glass vase that came with a bouquet of flowers but you've never used it again because you already have better, prettier vases? What about those 4 spatulas, 7 hot pad holders, 16 flashlights, and 22 pillowcases? What about those remote controls that stuck around even after the equipment they came with went out in the trash? Those computer parts that are obsolete? Those old phone wires, cable TV connectors, frayed extension cords? Is that pile of mail-order catalogs worth one more minute of your time? What do you own that's only worth the few seconds it will take to put it into the trash bag (black) or the donation bag (white) and stop it from using up another fraction of your life?

Stuff has a trade-off, and that trade-off is time. One spatula is worth the time it takes to clean it and store it because it's paying you back in return through its usefulness. But four spatulas? Now your time cost has gone up because not only do you have to clean them and store them, but you also have to spend time finding them (rustling through an overloaded kitchen tool drawer), making room for them (why won't this drawer close?), choosing between them (I use this one for pancakes but that one for hamburger patties), and maintaining them (this plastic handle feels like it might be coming loose).

At what point does the weight of that trade-off fall to the wrong side? Only you know the answer to that question, but when you can admit that *stuff* eats *time,* you can make the hard decisions that allow you to purge. In this world, there are many inequalities, such as income, opportunities, or education, but time is the great equalizer. Until we die, we all get exactly the same amount: 24 hours in a day.

Do you really want to keep wasting yours on *stuff?*

Making Hard Choices

With the trade-off questions in mind, you are now going to process *every* item in the area you have outlined and numbered on your Flow Plan. That means you are going to go through all closets, drawers, baskets, etc., in that one area and make a decision on every single thing, small and large, from the Tinies in the drawers to every piece of furniture, and *choose those things worth keeping.*

Everything else goes.

To get started, put a white trash bag in one clean garbage can and a black bag in the other. The reason you are using cans is to free up both hands to speed you along. Plastic bags flopped on the floor are inefficient and inconvenient because you have to reach over, pick them up, and hold them open when you want to put something in them. (That's also the reason I had you cut off the lid flaps from the cardboard boxes. The flaps get in the way and slow down your sorting.) You will be using the black bags for trash and the white bags for donations or garage sale items. Each time a bag gets full, pull it out, tie it off, and put in another one.

Next to the two lined trash cans, place your laundry basket or plastic bin. This is for items you run across that you are going to keep but that belong *in a specific place* in a different room. Every time this basket gets full, stop what you're doing, sort the items in the basket by room, carry those things to where they belong, and put them away. The size of the bin gives you a boundary (you can only stash stuff in the basket until it gets full), which prevents procrastination.

The cardboard boxes without lids are to be used as sorting tools and *not* for storage. The goals of sorting are twofold: giving things a place and getting a handle on duplicates.

The MAYBE boxes are for those items you know you should get rid of but can't make yourself do it. Whenever a MAYBE box gets full, tape it shut, stash it out of the way in the attic or basement, and mark a date on the calendar when you will make a decision about the contents of the box once and for all.

Giving Things a Place

Whenever you run across an item that you're going to keep but that item has no assigned "place" in your home, it goes into one of the cardboard sorting boxes. You've heard the old saying, "A place for everything and everything in its place"? This is true, and it needs to be one of your new mottos. One of the biggest causes of habitually messy houses is that items have been *acquired* but not *assigned*.

Assigning places is a deliberate act, which is difficult for the housekeeping impaired because it requires a certain type of focus that we may not naturally possess. Force yourself now to think about each item and where it can and should go in your home. (And resolve to do this from now on, for the rest of your life, for every single new thing you acquire. It's a wonderful habit to cultivate! Once you've made a decision on where an item goes, there's much less reason to leave it lying about.)

When choosing a place for a type of item, make sure that place is logical, convenient if it needs to be, or out of the way if it doesn't, and near the area where it will be used. Also be careful not to sub-sub-categorize things to such an extent that your organizational system is more trouble than it's worth.

Darnell has a place in his home that he calls the "Ticket Drawer." Originally it was established as a place to store airline tickets for upcoming trips so he wouldn't lose them by the time he needed them. Over the years, however, the Ticket Drawer has evolved so that it now includes not just tickets for upcoming travel or events, but also gift certificates, bonds, travel vouchers, etc. In other words, all pieces of paper that are worth money in and of themselves. If he created separate places for each of those different types of things, he would be over-organizing, which can be just as ineffective as not organizing at all. As it is, if any of those things comes in, he puts them in the Ticket Drawer, and if they go out, he takes them from the Ticket Drawer. Simple, isn't it?

As you toss your "homeless" items into your cardboard sorting boxes, do so in a fairly organized fashion. Assign to each box a category, and write that category on the outside with the permanent marker. Give yourself one box for "Miscellaneous," and the others use for categories that will vary depending on what types of things keep popping up. Some examples would be "Pet Supplies" (for leashes, pet brushes, nail clippers), "Beauty" (for barrettes, lipsticks, rollers), "Gifts," "Tools," "Electronics," "Toys." Or, if you prefer, label the boxes by where you think these items should end up, such as "Kitchen," "Garage," "Attic." That way the job of choosing a place is already half done by the time you get ready to deal with the items.

Depending on how quickly your boxes fill up, you can take care of giving these items a home whenever it feels right to you, whether that means after you have completed a single area, several areas, or the entire house. Just make sure you don't act too fast on items that may have duplicates, that you'll need for setting up Stations. (We'll go over Stations in chapter 14.) Duplicates are better dealt with when you have collected them from the entire house so you can see the total quantity you have to work with. For example, in our house we find it very handy to have four staplers, one each for my office, my husband's office, the kids' homework area, and the household paper-sorting area.

Getting a Handle on Tinies

If you recall from *Step 7,* Tinies are those small things that tend to pop up all over your house, such as writing implements, coins, paper clips, buttons. It is time to corral those little buggers once and for all, winnow them down, and assign them a place.

You have two choices about sorting your Tinies: Do it all at once or do it in two steps. Choose the method that works best for you.

If you do it all at once, take a wide but shallow cardboard box and fill it with as many individual plastic cups as you can fit in. Using your marker, label each cup ("crayons," "rubber bands," "twist ties," etc.), as shown.

When you run across Tinies, take a moment to drop each item into its correct cup. Do not redistribute these or put them where they belong until you have purged your entire house. By the time you are done, you may be astounded at the vast quantities you have of some items. Jerry's most fun surprise was coins. When he cashed in the coins he had collected from all over his house, it totaled almost $50. That's what I call a payoff!

If you'd rather deal with your Tinies in two steps (for me it was easier this way), skip the cups and toss all Tinies in the same box. Later, perhaps when you are watching television or looking for an easy project for the kids, take out this box and use the cups to sort the items further.

When I did this, I was astonished to see the sheer quantity of writing implements we possessed. I had my children further divide them into pencils, pens, colored pencils, markers, and crayons. When they were done, I felt a terrible surge of guilt thinking of schools in less affluent countries who would give anything to have half as many for an entire class. In the end, we kept about a fifth of what we owned, put the rest in Ziploc baggies, and donated them to a local nonprofit preschool and an after-school care center.

As you sort and purge throughout your house, you're probably also going to find that you own duplicates of a number of items such as scissors, staplers, and rulers. You don't need duplicates of most things, but don't automatically put every duplicate in the "donate" bag until you've made sure you don't need it for a Station.

Years ago, when I moved from one house to another and was forced to empty every closet, cabinet, and drawer, I was truly surprised to find that I owned multiples of many things from tweezers to dustpans, toothbrush holders to heating pads. Does this sound like you? If so, accept the fact that acquiring duplicates will probably always happen to some extent because it's the result of your inability to remember things you can't see. The best remedy for the duplicate problem is to assign a place to every new item you acquire as soon as you bring it into your home. That way when you go to put that item into its place, you'll see you already have one, and it won't be too late to return the new one.

Moving On

When you have completely finished decluttering an area, carry the trash to the outside cans, carry your white bags to the place reserved for donations and/or garage sale items, and move all cardboard sorting boxes to the next area on your Flow Plan. Cover them with the blanket, return to the area you just decluttered, and move on to the next step in that area.

My Most Embarrassing Messy House Story

—A Spit Take—

BY SASHA D.

My mother always had housekeepers when I was growing up, so no one ever taught me how to clean. Once I got married, my husband and I moved into a "fixer upper" that was pretty dirty, but I was stumped about how to get it clean. I decided to start in the kitchen, where I faced a filthy Formica counter. I knew I needed liquid, but it never crossed my mind to wet a rag at the sink or use some sort of spray cleaner.

Instead, all I could think to do was spit on the table and wipe it off. Just as I was spitting, I realized it probably wasn't a good idea. Too late! My husband walked into the kitchen at that moment and caught me. He was shocked! I've never gotten over the humiliation of being caught clueless when faced with a dirty tabletop.

12

Open Up and Clean

(CONVERT)

A wife of noble character who can find? She is worth far more than rubies....She sets about her work vigorously; her arms are strong for her tasks.

PROVERBS 31:10,17

Once an area has been decluttered and before you start choosing where items will go and putting them back, seize this opportunity to clean the area really well. Assemble a caddy with your most commonly used cleaning supplies so you don't have to run back to the cleaning closet every time you think of something else you need. Be sure to wipe, vacuum, and mop, eliminating all dust and grime from the space, including inside closets and cabinets and drawers. Some handy tools include:

- A "magic eraser"—Found in the cleaning aisle of your local store, these items really are like magic. If you've never tried one, get one now. Use on every single smudge, scuffmark, and hard-to-clean spot or streak you come across. The magic eraser will clean up more than you think!
- Multisurface cleaner—A good rule of thumb for any cleaning product is to *use the least powerful cleaner you can that still does the job.* Most multisurface cleaners are safe on a wide variety of surfaces. Be sure to read the

labels for more detailed information about which surfaces are safe to use with the product.

- A microfiber cloth—Professional cleaners have known about the wonderful cleaning characteristics of microfiber for a while, but the general consumer has been a bit slow in catching on. I used to hunt for these in the store (and didn't always find them), but lately they're popping up all over the place, even on a rack at my corner grocery. Because of the molecular structure of the fibers, microfiber does more of the work for you so that you need less elbow grease.

Later, we'll talk about how to organize your cleaning supplies for maximum efficiency. For now, it doesn't matter how you store them as long as you can easily get to them each time you reach this step for each area.

My Most Embarrassing Messy House Story

—Time for a Change—

BY EVELYN R.

Grandma dropped by for a scheduled visit. I'd cleaned and delegated jobs to the children, one of whom had forgotten to put away the vacuum cleaner. (This wasn't an issue; at least it proved we vacuumed on occasion!) The brand caught Grandma's eye, and she walked toward it and grasped the handle.

"Is this one of those light little 8-pound vacuums?" she asked.

I nodded and smiled just as Grandma tried to lift it—and couldn't.

"Good grief!" she cried. "That's a lot more than 8 pounds!"

I grabbed the handle. A churning in my stomach reminded me that I'd given all vacuuming responsibility to my 12-year-old, and

I hadn't checked the bag in ages. Gulping at the gritty gray trail of dust that followed any movement of the handle, I wrestled it to the front porch. It weighed at least 30 pounds! I unzipped the bag and engulfed my Grandma, Mom, and me in a cloud of dirt.

Grandma still laughs ten years later. The vacuum still works...if I remember to change the bag.

13

Neaten, Organize, and Solve Problem Spots

(CONVERT)

She watches over the affairs of her household and does not eat the bread of idleness. Her children arise and call her blessed; her husband also, and he praises her: "Many women do noble things, but you surpass them all."

PROVERBS 31:27-29

At this point, the clutter is gone, your area is clean, and now you are ready to turn your attention to making this space workable, attractive, and *self-cleaning.* This is where it gets fun! In your notebook, go back to the page where you listed the problems in this area and what you saw as their root causes. It's time to find and implement solutions.

Through the next six chapters, we'll go over the CONVERT steps you'll be doing throughout your home. But I'm only going to use area #1, your entryway, as the example. You will, of course, be doing every step of the CONVERT process in order, one area at a time, throughout your house. Only when one area has been fully converted do you move on to the next area.

So, using area #1 as the example, let's see how the general principles of the HTCI System can be applied.

An Example

The Messy Entryway

Let's say that the problems and root causes you have described for this area are:

- shoes lying around on floor—*kids too lazy to put them away where they belong*
- papers for school shoved on table—*if I file them away somewhere, I'll forget about them*
- car keys in a heap on counter—*we have a neat little row of hooks by the door, but nobody ever uses them*
- library books and videos piled by door—*I don't want to forget to take those to my car*
- backpacks and gym bags everywhere—*again, how hard can it be for the kids to walk around the corner and put these where they belong?*
- sports equipment scattered on floor—*I give up with these kids!*
- gloves and scarves on table—*I meant to put them away after I finished unloading the groceries, but I forgot*
- dirty footprints by door—*okay, so I don't mop as often as I should*
- doormat askew and looks messy—*maybe we need one of those rubber things that will hold it in place*
- fingerprints all over mirror beside door—*I'll take care of it when I do my weekly cleaning*
- plant in corner wilting from lack of water—*oops! forgot*

Separating these issues into categories, we can see that the four main problems are:

- *not putting stuff away where it belongs* (shoes lying around on floor, backpacks and gym bags everywhere, sports equipment scattered on floor, gloves and scarves on table)

- *no system for stuff that needs to go back out again* (car keys in a heap on counter, library books and videos piled by door)
- *no system for processing important papers* (papers for school shoved on table)
- *dirt and fingerprints are around until cleaning day* (dirty footprints by door, doormat askew and looks messy, fingerprints all over mirror beside door)

The good news is that every single one of these problems can be eliminated by applying House That Cleans Itself thinking. (In this section, we'll deal with the first three problems. The final problem, dirt and fingerprints, will be discussed when we get to chapter 17.)

Not Putting Stuff Away Where It Belongs

You can nag. You can try to remember. You can practice discipline or self-discipline all you want. Or, instead, why don't you fix the problem by adapting the house to fit the behavior?

Remember "a place for everything, and everything in its place"? If shoes, backpacks, gloves, and sporting equipment are being carried through the door and abandoned there, you need to relocate their "place" to somewhere very near that door. *Very* near. Like within a few steps.

If you're lucky, there's a coat closet right there—though if there is, right now it's probably filled with coats and jackets for all seasons, umbrellas, and other less-vital items. Now that you know what items need to be stored right by the door, take everything out of that closet and make it the home for the items that have been causing you problems now: shoes (use a floor rack or hanging shoe holder), backpacks (use heavy-duty hooks or a large, open container on the floor), gloves (we'll get to them in a minute), and the current sporting equipment (place on the top shelf or put in a tall bin or trash can). Just because it's called a coat closet doesn't mean it can only hold coats!

What if you're not so lucky and there's no storage close to the door? This was the problem Carly faced. Her solution was to buy a padded bench for holding backpacks and shoes and a small "jelly cabinet" for items waiting to go out the door. She didn't have a lot of room to work with, but she shopped around until she found two attractive pieces with the right dimensions to fit her entryway area.

For sporting equipment, she stopped it before it even came into the house by placing an all-weather storage bench on the porch just outside the door.

What if your main entryway is your kitchen, and it's already full of enough stuff? Sometimes it is true that no matter how hard you think outside the box in terms of adapting a house to fit a behavior, there comes a point where it's necessary to change the house as much as possible and then change the behavior to fit the limitations of the house.

In this case, perhaps the place for the shoes, backpacks, gloves, and sporting equipment can be moved to a cabinet right around the corner rather than two rooms away. Behaviors will still have to be changed, but at least by relocating the items' "home" closer to the door, putting that stuff where it belongs won't be quite as difficult as it was before.

For gloves and scarves, wherever they end up being kept, there is a set-up that can help them stay organized and easily at hand. (I wish I could remember where I first heard of this idea. I can't take credit for it myself!) Use a clear plastic or vinyl shoe organizer, the kind with pockets that hangs on the back of a door. (Mine has 24 pockets, and I bought it at a local discount store for $15.) Place a pair of gloves (and its matching scarf, if applicable) in each pocket. Clamp clothespins on several of the pockets for use with gloves that are damp. (Rather than shoving them into the plastic pocket, clamp them so they hang outside the pocket to dry first.) This creates a Winter Weather Station that's easy to use and tends to stay much neater than any other method I've seen.

What about the keys that had a place but the place wasn't being used? Believe it or not, in this world there are hook people and there are nonhook people. If the key hooks are not getting used, chances are it's because the nonhook people in the house subconsciously think it's too much trouble. (Nonhook people have to *focus* and *think* in order to use a hook, which distracts and confuses them for a moment, causing them to lose momentum. Over time they stop "seeing" hooks so they won't have to pause and think about using them.)

Replacing the hooks with a small basket might solve the problem. If there's no tabletop on which to place the basket, try using the kind of basket that hangs from the wall. Just make sure it's only big enough to hold keys and nothing else, or people might begin to "barnacle" it. You may be surprised at how a simple change—like switching from a hook to a basket—can eliminate the entire key problem.

So how do you know where an item's place should be? Whenever possible, store everything you own near where you use it most. Just as you wouldn't keep your frying pan in the bathroom, keeping your gift-wrapping supplies in the bedroom just because there's room in the closet doesn't make sense if you like to do your wrapping at the dining table. Using this kind of logic as the basis for your storage decisions keeps everything conveniently handy.

No System for Stuff That Needs to Go Out

Having a neat-but-effective launching pad is vital for the cleanliness of your entryway, and the more people you're launching on a daily basis, the more adaptable it needs to be.

Ideally, somewhere near the door should be a bookcase, cabinet, or shelving unit that holds as many baskets or bins as there are family members. (This needn't be unattractive. Many stylish, high-end stores sell units for just this purpose.) Each person uses his (or her) bin to place items he will need to take with him when he goes out again. For mom, that might be her purse, sunglasses, and library books; for dad, outbound mail or dry cleaning; for kids, lunchboxes, school papers, and class projects.

If these bins are located near the door, using them is not a difficult habit to cultivate at all. Just make sure the shortest members of your family can reach the bins that have been assigned to them. If your entryway is in a less visible area, for example your family goes in and out of the house primarily through a mudroom, you may prefer to use open cubbies or clear bins rather than the more decorative ones you would use near a front door. That way everyone can see their items and will be less likely to forget them. The whole "out of sight, out of mind" issue has always been one of my biggest problems with regard to being launched. Opaque bins or baskets simply didn't work for me because I would forget to look inside and take out the items I needed for the day. Clear baskets were the solution!

Because of her need to be able to see the items she is supposed to take with her, Carly has set up her launching pad in the jelly cabinet that sits beside her front door. Everyone has been given his or her own shelf inside the cabinet, and Carly applied adhesive cork to the inside of the cabinet door so that extra reminders could be pinned there like on a bulletin board. Most of the time Carly leaves the door open so everyone can see their stuff and have their memories jogged. If company comes a knockin', all they do is shut the door to that cabinet and their entryway instantly looks neat.

No System for Processing Important Papers

Do you have a household paper-processing system that works for you? If not, you're not alone. How to handle and process the paper that comes into our lives is a tremendous challenge for most people, and it gets more complex every year. The digital age, despite all predictions, has increased the paper load, not decreased it.

To get a handle on the paper in your house, first consider the various ways it comes in:

- through the mailbox
- from your children (carried home from school and organizations)
- from your office (brought home by you)
- from your spouse (brought home by him or her)
- from your activities, such as church bulletins and gym schedules
- from possessions you acquire, such as warranties and receipts
- other, such as sale ads you pick up, menus delivered with food, and flyers left at your door

If papers came from only one source at one time, they would be much easier to contain. Once a day we could simply receive our pile and deal with it. But it's the dribbling in here and there that throws us off. *If you are not a procrastinator,* you might find it easier to deal with paper by dumping every single thing that comes into your home into a conveniently placed box or bin and then processing it all at one time, every day, at the same time each day. If, however, a box with papers in it is something you know you might not get around to on a daily basis, *don't use this system.* Before you know it, the box will be overflowing and the electric company will turn your power off.

Instead, try the two-step sort system that works in my house. I designed this after understanding that I was a round peg in a square world, and the systems that worked for most people were never going to click with me. My attempts at filing have always been dismal failures, so I finally came up with my two-step sort system: 1) "Quick Sort"—done whenever a paper comes into my hands, and 2) "Slow Sort"—done at the end of every week. Both steps are described in detail in Part 3, "Doing the Paper Two-Step." Using these two steps in combination will eliminate the paper problem in your house for good.

Ditch the Time-Suckers

Before we move on to the next step, you may be wondering if there are any House That Cleans Itself principles we can apply to the messy doormat and the thirsty plant. I'm glad you asked!

A doormat that won't stay neatly in place needs to be repaired or replaced. Throughout your house, over time, look into replacing any items that need repeated "fixing" to keep from looking messy. From couches with pillow backs (never, ever, buy a couch with moveable pillows for the back unless you want to waste minutes of every day straightening them) to miniblinds that don't want to hang straight, from dust ruffles that are frayed or torn to clothes that no longer fit, when you tolerate these faulty possessions you become a victim of their time-consuming imperfections. As soon as you can, fix them or get rid of them. Life's too short and your time is too valuable to waste.

As for the rug in that entryway, try putting one of those rubber rug mats underneath. If that doesn't solve the problem, relegate that slippery mat to a different spot in your home (see if it will stay put on some other floor surface, such as carpet or tile). If that doesn't work, get rid of it. When you buy a new mat, make sure it won't slip and that it has a textured pile to attract dirt.

For the plant, you have several choices:

- convert the plants in your house to fakes
- assign a more reliable member of the family as the plant caretaker
- make your plants self-watering. There are a variety of self-watering devices on the market, including self-watering containers (they have a reservoir in the bottom and use wicking material to slowly draw the water up to the plant), and water-retaining crystals, watering balls, water-absorbing mats. Check online for "self-watering plants" or visit a local gardening center for more information.

- get a "canary in a coal mine." Shari has a small plant in her entryway that begins to droop the moment it gets thirsty, thus serving as a visible reminder to water all of the plants in her house.

As you can see, turning a messy entryway into an entryway that cleans itself involves:

- listing the problems that usually pop up in that area
- identifying the root causes of those problems
- applying creative solutions to prevent and eliminate those problems forever

Simply put, we are anticipating messes *before* they start.

My Most Embarrassing Messy House Story

—No Rest for the Weary—

BY LYNN G.

My house is a clutter pit. Paperwork is laid out everywhere. It's been several years since I last saw the floors in my teenagers' rooms.

My typical modus operandi for holidays is to clean and then stack piles of paperwork and things I have no place to stow, such as candles, magazines, folders, large photographs, coupons, and free samples, on our bed the morning of the event. That way, no matter how messy the bedrooms are, when relatives arrive for festivities, the part of the house they see looks clutter-free.

One Thanksgiving my brother-in-law, who lives an hour away, pulled an all-nighter at work and was exhausted. He approached me to ask if there was a quiet place he could take a quick nap after dinner. How could I explain my five-bedroom house had no beds available?

Red-faced, I had to double-stack junk on one side of our bed in order to clear off a spot on the other side for him to sleep.

14

Verify Rabbit Trails and Set Up Stations

(CONVERT)

Moreover, when God gives any man wealth and possessions, and enables him to enjoy them, to accept his lot and be happy in his work—this is a gift of God.

ECCLESIASTES 5:19

A rabbit trail is what you go on when you need to do a recurring task but the items required to do that task are not stored together. Sometimes you have to wander through several rooms—or even the whole house—to gather your supplies. That gathering takes time and energy and serves to create mess, especially if you don't always put those items back where you got them.

One of the most irritating rabbit trails I used to go on regularly came up whenever I wanted to write someone a letter, send a card, or mail a package. In my house this used to be a monumental task—one that I usually ended up avoiding entirely—because the things I needed for doing it were all over the place.

The *stationery* was in my home office. The pretty stationery, however, was in my bedside table in the bedroom because I thought I might pen letters in the evenings while my husband read a book or worked a crossword. (I never ended up doing this, but that's beside the point. The idea seemed lovely, and I still held on to the hope that I might.)

The box of *envelopes* was either in the home office upstairs, where I kept office supplies, or in the kitchen downstairs because I frequently needed envelopes for sending various papers back and forth to the kids' schools. Pens were everywhere, but the *special pen* I preferred to use when writing something was either in the bottom of my purse or in whatever room I had been in when I used it last.

The *thank-you cards* were usually somewhere in one of my daughters' rooms, more than likely under the bed because no matter how bad I am about taking the time to send thank-you notes, for some reason I've always been fairly good about making my kids do it.

Greeting cards were in abundance (we who are "housekeeping impaired" tend to hang on to unused greeting cards for years, knowing that eventually the occasion will arise to use each and every one of them), but the box where we stashed the cards was so crammed full that many were bent or ragged, the matching-sized envelopes were in a separate box, and it was time consuming to go through all those cards to find the right one for the right occasion.

The perpetual *calendar* where we recorded the birthdays and special dates of friends and family members was somewhere in one of my husband's "to be filed" piles. The *packing tape* was in the utility closet, and the *bigger envelopes, boxes, and address labels* were in my office. Finally, *postage stamps* were in a basket on the front hall table, except for the *stamps of unusual postage amounts,* which were in a cubbyhole in an organizer in the dining room.

Needless to say, what should have been a quick and simple process was a nightmare. No wonder I was so lax at correspondence! (Did you think I was kidding when I said I'm not naturally gifted at housekeeping?)

Strangely, it never occurred to me how inefficient this whole system was until a local store had a two-for-the-price-of-one sale on envelopes. I came home with two boxes, both of which I put in my upstairs office where envelopes were supposed to go. One of those boxes soon got carried downstairs because I needed an envelope to send in the kids' lunch money. Eventually it dawned on me that having two boxes of envelopes—one upstairs and one down—was saving me a lot of time. My thinking escalated from there into a giant "Duh!" and a slap on the forehead. That very day I gathered up every single item related to this particular rabbit trail, put them all in one place, and never had to go on a rabbit trail to write a letter again.

Turning Rabbit Trails into Stations

In a house that cleans itself, all rabbit trails are identified and then eliminated. How? By establishing Stations. First you gather the items for the task. Then put all the items into a container, such as a basket or bin. Clearly label that container and put it into a nearby cabinet or closet. You want these items close and easy to access. But you also don't want that container cluttering a countertop or table surface.

Whatever your rabbit trails, the key to solving all of them involves three steps:

1. All of the needed items are identified and collected.
2. This collection needs to be placed *in a single container* in an appropriate storage area (such as a cabinet or drawer) *in the room where you are most likely to perform this task.*
3. Any of the collected items that might also be needed for performing other tasks in other locations *should be duplicated whenever you can afford to do so* and placed in the different places they'll be used.

This third step shows why it's important to figure out these rabbit trails *prior* to purging your clutter but not to set up "Stations" until *after* purging your clutter. Most organizational experts tell you that you need only one stapler, not four, or only one good pair of scissors, not ten bad ones. I beg to differ! Messy people will grab the stuff they need from wherever they can most easily find it, cart it off to use on some project in another room, and never put it back where it came from. Since a HTCI provides the tools a person needs to do what they need to do in the area they need to do it in, you are going to want to hang on to some of the duplicates that turn up when purging your clutter to use in setting up Stations.

The whole reason for having a duplication of items elsewhere is so that the people in your house will use those—and leave the items in your Station alone.

The Rabbit Trails in Your Life

There are many common Rabbit Trails that may be eating up time and making a mess in your house. Let's identify some of them. Turn to a fresh page in your notebook and list all rabbit trails you can think of, starting with *writing a letter/sending a card,* if that's an issue for you.

Don't go overboard by listing activities you rarely do or do only a few times a year. But any sort of task that sends you rooting around the house for the related tools at least once a month should be noted.

Using a separate page for each rabbit trail, write down the items you need to assemble to turn those rabbit trails into Stations.

Where will all of these items go? Each "group" of items goes into a separate container. These containers will usually be tucked away into closets, drawers, and cabinets in different rooms in your house, depending on where you perform the activities the items are for. When will you set up these Stations? As you're implementing the conversion process, when you get to the rooms that need Stations, you'll assemble them then. That's why this process is gradual and begins on paper. Making these lists before creating the Stations helps you know what to look for as you're working in other rooms (you might already have the items needed) and keeps you working only in one room at a time. This keeps the process logical and efficient. Once you have a list of the Stations you need and the items that will go in each Station, the hard part is done. The rest is a piece of cake...or maybe I should say a bunch of carrots.

Here are some common Stations you may want to establish in your home, along with suggestions for what they might contain.

Making a Phone Call

Twenty years ago all people required at their Phone Stations were a personal address book and the telephone book that came from the phone company. Nowadays you need a lot more than that!

You may need the *white pages, the yellow pages, your church directory, your school directories,* and a variety of *phone lists,* such as your company employee list, the snow-closing call list for your preschool, and the team rosters from your kids' various sports teams. To make matters more complicated, there's a good chance your cell phone contains numbers you haven't written down anywhere else, such as your kids' friends' cell phones or that Chinese restaurant you pass on the way home from work.

Gather all these items. If you don't use a BlackBerry, PDA, or something similar, compile a *list of your most frequently called numbers* in a Rolodex, address book, or notebook. You'll update this list on a regular basis (including making note of those numbers on your cell phone). My list is in a word processing file on my laptop. I amend and append the list all the time. It includes the numbers of friends, family members, our doctors, the businesses we frequent, the repair services we use, local establishments such as the library and the post office, and all of my kids' friends' home phones/cell phones/parents' cell phones. *Whew!* Currently my list runs seven tightly spaced pages. Keeping it up-to-date saves me an enormous amount of time and trouble. Maybe I *should* invest in a BlackBerry!

If there's more than one phone in your house, especially if the others aren't portable, create more than one Telephone Station. If this seems like overkill to you, don't do it. You know where and how your family uses the phone(s) in your home. Our house has three, which means I always ask for three copies of each phone book from the phone company, get three copies of our church and school directories, and make duplicates of all those phone lists we're given so there's one for each Phone Station. The loose lists and my personal list, which I print out every few months to keep the hard copies up to date, are kept in a narrow (½-inch) *3-ring binder* at each Phone Station. (Also in the binder are menus for local takeout and delivery restaurants.) That means each Phone Station also has a *hole punch* and a pack of *hole reinforcers,* so it's easy to add a new page to the notebook and keep it neat.

The final element that every Phone Station needs, unless you live alone, is a *telephone message book.* Get one that records messages in duplicate. I'm talking about the "While You Were Out" kind they use in businesses, which can be purchased at any office supply store for less than $10. (Mine are spiral bound, come three to a page, and cost $5.49 at Staples.) If you, your spouse, or your kids take phone messages for each other, you need one of these. Phone messages are recorded on the top page, torn off, and placed on the fridge under a magnet. (Actually, for about two dollars more, you can buy the kind that have temporary adhesive on the back so no magnet is needed.) If that paper gets lost, there's always a duplicate copy in the notebook. These message books have worked better for us than any whiteboard, bulletin board, or other system we've tried.

Making a Pot of Coffee

If you're in the habit of making coffee, it stands to reason that *everything you need should be in the cabinet nearest your coffeemaker.* This includes *mugs, cups, saucers, sugar, sweetener, nondairy creamer, coffee, filters, measuring scoop,* and anything else that's part of your coffee routine. For stirring, keep a few *extra teaspoons* in the same cabinet so you don't have to go to the silverware drawer or buy a box of *plastic stirrers* (about $4 for a pack of 1000) at a discount or office supply store.

I'm not much of a coffee person, but my oldest daughter likes to drink a cup on the way to high school. Therefore our Coffee Station also includes *Styrofoam cups with matching plastic lids* so she can make her coffee to go.

Doing Homework

Most kids gravitate to the place where they like doing homework best. My girls rotate between the kitchen table, the computer desk, and the big comfy chair in the family room, depending on what sort of homework they're doing.

I used to feel guilty that they didn't have neat matching desks in their bedrooms, well lit and filled with the latest office and art supplies. Not anymore! The more I read about successful homework routines and strategies, the more I'm convinced that most kids do best when they can work in a fairly quiet and peaceful environment *with a parent nearby.* All those years I felt guilty they were doing their homework at the kitchen table as I cooked dinner, but as it turns out, we were on the right track. According to many experts, that's one of the best setups going.

Wherever your kids do their homework, establish a Homework Station that's easily accessible to that place. Depending on the ages of your kids, a Homework Station may include all sorts of *school supplies,* such as lined paper, white paper, pens, pencils, colored pencils, markers, crayons, glue sticks, tape, white-out or correction tape, a 3-hole punch, hole reinforcers, extra folders and spiral notebooks, notecards, calculator, construction paper, stapler, staples, highlighters, Post-it Notes, dictionary, thesaurus, study Bible, and foreign language dictionary. Work with your children to find out what they need, but *don't oversupply them.* If the Homework Station is too cluttered with things they don't need, you'll end up with another mess.

Depending on how much stuff is required, you may be able to keep everything in a tote bag or you may end up filling several shelves in a cabinet or bookshelf. As long as you stock everything your kids need but nothing they don't, you'll be in good shape.

The only homework-related items I don't keep in the Homework Station are poster boards and foamcore boards, which are stored behind a bookshelf in my office so they won't get bent or used wastefully. Otherwise, the kids' Homework Station is located in three drawers in a bureau in our family room. The kids are in charge of keeping an inventory and letting me know whenever something needs to be replaced.

Charging Electronic Appliances

You need to locate your Charging Station near an *outlet* that's out-of-the-way so you won't have to look at it or bump into it all the time. However, it also must be near enough to the center of action that family members will walk over and plug in their cameras, iPods, cell phones, etc. The closer this place is to the main door your family usually goes in and out of, the better.

I have seen some nifty "Charging Stations" in mail order catalogs, but they always seem a little pricy for something that's essentially a plastic box with wire holes in the back. Since we keep ours in the kitchen, I made our Charging Station out of a breadbox by drilling a hole in the lower back. I placed a surge-protected power strip inside and ran the cord out the hole in the back to the outlet. When we need to, we lift the breadbox lid, plug in our devices, and close the lid. (This could also be done with a lidded basket or other container.) Our charging devices are still handy, but the messy wires are hidden from view.

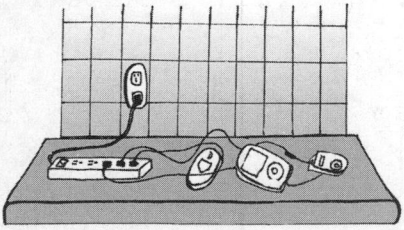

Whether you buy a Charging Station or make your own, if you have young kids make sure these "hot" cords are out of reach and fastened securely. You don't want your children to get zapped by electricity!

My family has also found that it helps to have duplicates of some chargers to use for travel. These I clearly labeled and keep in a plastic bin in the luggage closet. Whenever we travel we pull the chargers from there rather than messing up our nifty kitchen Charging Station. It's worth the cost of the extra chargers just to get folks to leave the Station setup alone.

Paying Bills and Balancing the Checkbook

What tools do you use when you sit down to pay bills? Where do you like to do it? Whether you sit at a home desk or prefer to spread out on the kitchen or dining table, everything you need should be together in one station. If you have a good system for tracking and paying your bills but the postage stamps are in another room, you are wasting time when you have to stop what you're doing, get up, and go get them.

If you're a "table" bill-payer, make sure your Station items are placed in a portable container that can be stowed in a nearby cabinet or closet and is easily accessible. Here are some items for your bill-paying process.

A receptacle for incoming bills and bank statements, whether you prefer a single container, a 31-day expanding file folder, or a multi-slot wooden sorter (with bills placed by due date). You will be putting the bills into this container each week when you do your Slow Sort (described in Part 3, "Doing the Paper Two-Step"), so it needs to be at an accessible and convenient height and location.

A *computer.* Obviously, I'm not telling you to stash an extra computer in the closet just for bill-paying time. But if you're a table bill-payer, I am suggesting you stash in your Station whatever else you might need to use with that computer, such as an extension cord, a power strip, and printer paper so your set-up is as quick and convenient as possible.

A *calculator or adding machine.* Are you a "calculator martyr," wasting time pressing the tiny little keys of the free one that came with your last wallet? Stop! You need a tabletop model, preferably an electric one, with a full-size keyboard. Don't forget to include an *extension cord* in your Station if needed.

Other items you may include are *blank checks, envelopes, postage stamps, a letter opener,* and *pens.* From an office supply store, pick up *a self-inking "Paid" stamp* (one that leaves space for date paid and payment method). Read "Doing the Paper Two-Step" in Part 3 to learn what to do with bills once they're paid.

One final note about your bill-paying area. A major part of reducing clutter is to stop it before it gets there. To that end, I highly recommend using online bill-paying as much as possible or at least for those bills paid in the same amount each month, such as your mortgage or car payment. Edward is not the most tech-savvy person around, but he made a point of learning how to do this (the bank will teach you), and he is now saving time and preventing the clutter of more paperwork every single month. Bills still come in the mail, but Edward looks forward to the day when the entire process, from billing to payment, will be done electronically without a paper in sight.

Wrapping Gifts

Your Gift-Wrapping Station can be as simple or elaborate as your gift-wrapping is. For years I used scissors, a roll of tape, and the Sunday comics. Nowadays, though I'm not a gift-wrap fanatic like some of my more artsy friends, I do take a pass on the comics in favor of pretty *wrapping paper* and curling *ribbon* or *gift bags and tissue paper.* The key is to put everything together in one place: *gift wrap, tape, scissors* (that are used only here and never carted off), *labels* or *tags,* and a *permanent marker.*

Whatever you do, if you are housekeeping impaired resist the temptation to hoard tiny scraps of wrapping paper in anticipation of wrapping a really small box. Paper scraps belong in the trash or recycle bin even if they're pretty. Also make a habit of tossing any wrapping paper that gets crushed or bent. If it's too raggedy to use on a gift, why hang on to it?

Getting Ready for Church

This may seem like an unusual item to include, but think about that mad, last-minute Sunday morning rush when you can't find your Sunday school book or your son's Bible or your tithing envelopes. I truly believe that one of Satan's favorite tools to use against Christian families is to make chaos out of our mornings when we are trying to get ready for church. Those dumb little arguments that spring up as we run around preparing to leave can result in irritated parents, sullen kids, and hearts that are in no way ready for worshiping or learning.

For the next month, as your family gets ready for church, pay attention to the items that are causing problems. Include those in a Church-Going Station. You'll probably end up with a mix of *emergency items* that can be used in a pinch, such as an extra hairbrush, a new pack of pantyhose or knee-highs, a pair of men's black socks, and a spare Bible. Include in this Station your *Sunday school books, tithing envelopes, blank checks,* and a *pen.*

There is one more consideration for the at-home mom or dad or someone who works in a job where daily clothing is casual. If this is you, chances are that in a typical week you're going to dress better on Sunday morning than you do the other six days. Even if you go to a church that tends toward casual dress, you're still probably going to wear your better casual dress items, such as slacks rather than jeans, and button-down shirts rather than T-shirts. For folks who dress up to go into an office each day, getting dressed for church is no big deal. But if you spend most of your week in shorts or sweat pants or tattered jeans, and you're not in the daily habit of dressing up, you need to pay extra attention to being ready for Sunday mornings before they arrive.

Organizational experts talk a lot about laying out the next day's clothes each evening, to which I roll my eyes and say that only organized people can remember to do that. (Hey, more power to you if you've made this a habit!) But here's what the rest of us can do. When you get home from church on Sunday, as you change into something more comfortable, go ahead and pick your outfit for *next* Sunday. I mean everything, including outerwear, underwear, socks, shoes, and jewelry. Put the entire ensemble someplace where it won't get wrinkled or disturbed between now and then.

For my Sunday Dressing Station I use a cheap, clear-plastic, extra-long hanging bag that zips up the front and has an outer pocket for shoes. Each week I place next Sunday's outfit in the bag, carefully put the jewelry and other clothing items in the bottom, and zip it shut. I put the shoes in the outer pocket. I hang the whole thing at the far end of my closet. When Sunday rolls around, all I have to do is pull it out and I'm ready to get dressed. Not only can I find everything I need, this also prevents those Sunday-morning surprises when all the nice clothes are wrinkled or I can't find the scarf that pulls an outfit together.

If you can't find such a hanging bag or don't want to spend the money, try this handy solution. You'll need a hole punch or scissors, a permanent marker, three big zipper-locked baggies, and a nice wooden or plastic hanger. Label the three plastic bags "Shoes," "Jewelry," and "Other," and then punch or cut a hole in each bag, about an inch below the zipping line, in the center.

When you prepare your clothes for the next Sunday, hang the outfit on the hanger, put the other items in their designated bags, zip the bags shut, and run the top of the hanger through the holes.

You'll now be ready for Sunday when it rolls around! Just be sure to hang your Sunday ensemble out of the way so you won't be tempted to use any of those items during the week.

You can also use this idea for costumes and special dress-up events.

Getting Ready for a Workout

There's a good reason you need to set up this Station: If your workout involves no necessary prep time, like gathering stuff for your gym bag or finding your favorite exercise tape, you'll be more likely to follow through. How many times have you skipped a workout because it was too much trouble to pull things together?

If you workout solely at a gym or the Y, your gym bag *is* your Workout Station. Make sure that it includes all *personal equipment* you need, such as *goggles, earplugs, swim cap, towel, water bottle, lock for the locker.* Be sure to include items you need for showering and doing your hair and makeup so you never have to grab those things from your shower and dressing area at home. I can't tell you how many years I spent with one bottle of deodorant shuttled back and forth between gym bag and bathroom until I finally had one of those forehead-slapping, "Duh!" moments. It's amazing how having two bottles of deoderant has made my life so much simpler!

To keep your Workout Station current, make a habit of replacing certain items as soon as you get home from the gym, such as towel, water bottle, clean socks and underwear, rather than waiting until it's time to go again. That way your gym bag is ready to go at a moment's notice.

If you do your workouts at home, your Workout Station may involve *equipment* such as a treadmill, free weights, or simply the *television, exercise tapes,* and *open floor space.* If you do your exercising outside, you might use a good pair of *sneakers, a portable radio, a tennis racket, a can of balls, a basketball, a volleyball, a hockey stick,* and *a pair of skates.*

Whatever your home equipment needs are, be sure to think through your *entire* workout. Remember to include *every* item you might need, such as *extra batteries* for your *CD player, Band-Aids* for blisters, a *knee or ankle brace* if needed, an *air pump* for your basketball or bicycle tires, a *water bottle, a visor, sports sunglasses,* and *sunscreen.* Depending on how much room this Station takes up, you may end up using anything from a small tote bag to an entire closet.

To keep outdoor sporting equipment from overtaking your home, establish two distinct areas: your *Workout Station,* which holds your current sporting equipment and supplies, and your *Sporting Goods Storage,* which holds the equipment you use at other times during the year. Your Sporting Goods Storage needs to be easily accessible, such as in a garage or shed, but out of the way of general traffic. This is especially important if you are heavily involved in winter sports and summer sports. Skis, sleds, snowboards, and other equipment can take up an enormous amount of room and should be stored far out of the way in the off-season. My husband keeps our skis and sleds above the garage, stacked along the rafters, until the first snowflakes fall.

Even if you're good about putting away the off-season equipment, you still may have trouble accommodating all of the current stuff. One resourceful mother I know solved her problem of having three sons in three different sports in a very clever way. Because each kid needed his own Workout Station, she bought three full-sized metal lockers. She put the lockers in a row in the garage, right beside the door, and told the boys their in-use and available equipment could not exceed the interior space of the lockers. That forced them to weed out bulky, off-season items such as hockey sticks and football pads and move them to the sporting goods storage area when they weren't in use. The locker system worked so well that eventually she added a fourth locker. The bottom portion was used to store the air pump and other communal items they played with in their yard year-round, such as a basketball, a softball, and a bat. The top portion was reserved for her own Workout Station, which consisted primarily of a helmet, pads, and a pair of roller blades. Once she no longer had to dig around the garage and the shed to pull her things together, she used them far more often.

Getting Ready to Travel

As a family we travel so much that we have dedicated an entire closet as our Travel Station. It holds all of our suitcases and sleeping bags. Inside is also a plastic shelving unit with clear, removable bins that contain duplicate *chargers* for our cell phones and cameras, *travel-sized toiletries* (usually extras brought home from hotels), *tote bags, luggage tags and straps,* a variety of cloth and plastic *zippered bags* (most acquired over the years from getting free gifts from the Clinique counter), disposable *cameras,* two different-sized boxes of *baggies,* nifty *travel tools* like a small *portable fan,* an *adapter kit,* a *travel alarm clock,* and more.

Our maps, atlases, and travel books are kept in a different place, as are our passports, so not every item we need for travel is in that one closet, but we have been able to come pretty close! Certainly getting ready for a trip is much easier than it used to be.

If you hardly ever travel, you may not need a Travel Station. On the other hand, if you or a family member travel constantly, take your Travel Station to the next level and keep a *packed bag* in your closet at all times. I know one woman who is a professional speaker and author who has engagements and appearances 30 to 40 weekends per year. Her bag is literally never unpacked. As soon as she returns from one trip, she replaces any used-up items in her bag, packs it with the clothes she'll need for her next trip, and then puts it into the closet. At the end of the week, when it's time for her to leave again, she can grab her bag, add any last-minute items, and go. The reason this works for her is because she buys clothes that are specifically made not to wrinkle. I didn't really believe there were such things until she convinced me to buy one wrinkle-free outfit for myself. Now I'll never travel with anything else! Surf the web for "wrinkle-free clothing," and you'll find a number of options from a variety of suppliers.

Making Small Household Repairs

Chances are your home has two "levels" of tools: the everyday stuff, such as hammers and screwdrivers, and the more involved stuff like band saws and miters. Most folks, even messy folks, are fairly organized about these bigger tools and are able to keep track of them because the tools are unlikely to get carried to other places around the house. (My kids may unthinkingly run off with my tape measure, but I doubt they'll ever misplace the chain saw.)

It's not difficult to set up a Heavy-Duty Tool Area in a garage or shed and then duplicate some of the minor tools for an Indoor Repair Station. What that Repair Station includes depends entirely on how handy you are and how likely you are to want at your fingertips mid-level tools such as *drills* and *electric screwdrivers*.

In my house, my husband handles everything more complicated than hammering in a nail. He likes to keep his tools together in one place, so all I have in our Repair Station are duplicate items of the most common things, including a *hammer;* an assortment of *screwdrivers* (big and small, Phillips and regular); an assortment of *nails, screws, hooks, picture hangers; a carpenter's measure; a small level; and a roll of duct tape.* Your Repair Station may be more thorough than mine, but the key is to fill it only with the items you will use regularly and none of the things you only need two or three times a year.

Keeping Your Stations Stocked

One final note: After you have created your Stations, if you find the items are still being carried off, don't hesitate to nip the problem in the bud:

- Use a permanent marker to *label the items by their Station,* just as people do in busy offices where fellow employees inadvertently take things from desks and never return them. For example, you might label one pair of scissors: *Gift-Wrapping Station. Do not remove!*

- Have a talk with the "thieves" and *establish penalties* for misappropriation of Station items.
- *Choose a less visible area* for that Station (for example, a bottom side drawer rather than top center drawer) so there is less temptation to pull from it.
- *Tie items down.* After years of battling with my daughters, who were forever stealing my best hairbrush, I tied one end of a long piece of yarn to the hairbrush and the other end to a dresser knob. It didn't look very good, and it was irritating to brush my hair that way, but over the next few weeks the string helped my girls become more aware of the fact they were grabbing the brush and walking away as they were using it. Once that lesson was firmly established and their habit broken, I removed the string.

Do whatever it takes to keep your Stations intact. You'll find that creating and maintaining Stations saves you an enormous amount of time and energy!

My Most Embarrassing Messy House Story

—The Tale of the Missing Vandals—

BY PETER M.

One night my roommate and I went to the movies. While we were gone, some friends came over to our apartment to hang out. When they realized we weren't at home, they thought it would be funny to play a joke on us. They put all of our furniture on the front porch in a big, upside-down pile, and left a "ha ha" note on the door. Unfortunately that note blew away before we got back.

When we came home we didn't realize a joke was played. We thought we had been vandalized. Scared to go inside, we called the police. They came and entered the apartment, searching throughout for signs of vandalism. When they came back out, they announced that the vandals were gone now but obviously they had been inside the apartment and torn it apart.

"You'll have to come in and make a full report," they told us. "There are clothes all over, papers, all kinds of stuff. They totally destroyed the place."

When we went in, we found no one had been inside at all. The disastrous mess the cops talked about was the mess we lived in every day!

15

Examine Sight Zones

(CONVERT)

The LORD has rewarded me according to my righteousness, according to my cleanness in his sight.

2 SAMUEL 22:25

Go to your area #1 and stand at the doorway, facing in, as if you had just stepped into the house. Now look from side to side. Your Sight Zone includes all of the parts of the room(s) you can see. When you consider the Sight Zone for the space you are in, ask yourself if there is anything you need to do to make this first impression of the interior of your home more attractive and easier to keep clean. Does the area "work" in terms of setup, flow, and design? Are there any changes you can make, such as touching up chipped paint, replacing shabby or overworn items, or removing a stubborn stain?

In a House That Cleans Itself, you give your home the appearance of being cleaner than it is by carefully directing the eye toward the stay-neat areas.

Consider, also, how many other rooms you can see from where you are standing. Is your Sight Zone too broad, covering so many areas that it's impossible to keep them all looking nice all the time?

In the suburbs of Philadelphia where I live, big, brand-new houses are popping up almost as frequently as dandelions. Apparently designed by people who've never had to keep a busy house clean, most of these places feature front door Sight Zones that encompass several rooms, including the kitchen and a big family room. If the houses are nicely decorated and perfectly neat, the broad scope of the Sight Zone is very effective. But more often than not, from what I've seen, if there's even a little bit of clutter in the family room and a few dirty dishes by the sink, the whole beautiful effect of the home is ruined. The house looks messy.

Now, honestly, unless your home happens to be spotless all the time, why is having such broad Sight Zones worth it? In a House That Cleans Itself, you give your home the appearance of being cleaner than it is by carefully directing the eye toward the stay-neat areas.

If your entryway offers a view into too many rooms, establish various "concealers" to redirect the view. The most effective concealing is done by architectural changes, such as building a wall or putting doors on previously open doorways. If you implement architectural changes that will limit the view from your doorway, make sure your welcome area is nicely decorated and doesn't seemed cramped. You also don't want to block the flow of your home. But dealing with your Sight Zone will greatly reduce your housekeeping stress and increase your home's positive first impression.

If I lived in a house where everyone who came to my front door could see at a single glance all of the rooms where my family cooks, eats, and relaxes, I would probably go crazy with cleaning. I'd never relax enough to enjoy my own home. Either that or I'd fall to the other extreme and give up on cleaning entirely, frustrated that even when my house was clean, one little area of clutter could make the whole place look messy. So redirect and limit the view so your house can seem spotless from the front door but be as lived in as you need it to be further inside. Life is messy sometimes, especially when it's creative or delicious or fun, so don't let a poor Sight Zone hinder your family's activities.

If architectural changes are too extreme for you, create a concealer by using:

- a big piece of furniture in the sight line, turning it in such a way that it doesn't block the flow but directs the view away from the rest of the house
- an angled mirror, which will also make the entry space look larger
- a folding screen
- plants, perhaps on a tall plant stand or hanging from the ceiling
- a beautiful curtain
- a trellis
- some combination of all of the above

Your creativity is only limited by the design of your home and what sort of space your welcome area includes.

Beyond the Entryway

Despite what you may be thinking, the main reason for establishing clean Sight Zones isn't to impress the deliveryman or the neighbor who never comes any further than the front door. First and foremost, it's to impact *you and everyone else who lives there* every time you go in or out. When you walk through a door and come upon a mess, you feel demoralized. When you walk through a door and see clean, even if it's just a first impression, you feel in control and energized. That's why Sight Zones apply to entryways to every single room in your house. (Rooms with multiple entrances have multiple Sight Zones.)

Anything in your home that's likely to get messy looking over time should be placed outside the Sight Zone.

Say, for example, that your family tends to be careless when it comes to bookshelves. They grab books and use them, but they don't put them back as neatly as they should. After a while, half of the books are no longer neatly lined on the shelves. They're crammed in sideways and piled on top. In a House That Cleans Itself, the first step is to see if you can come up with some way that the bookshelf can be changed to accommodate that behavior. That could mean weeding out some of the books so the shelves aren't quite so packed or maybe getting more bookends so it's easier to keep the books neatly arranged. You could also replace your open shelving with cabinets, but that's a fairly expensive change you may not want to make. You could—and should—try changing the behavior, but as we've learned, behavior isn't likely to stay changed for the long term.

So invoke "the rule of the Sight Zone," which states that anything in your home that's likely to get messy looking over time should be placed outside the Sight Zone. Picture the same room set up two different ways:

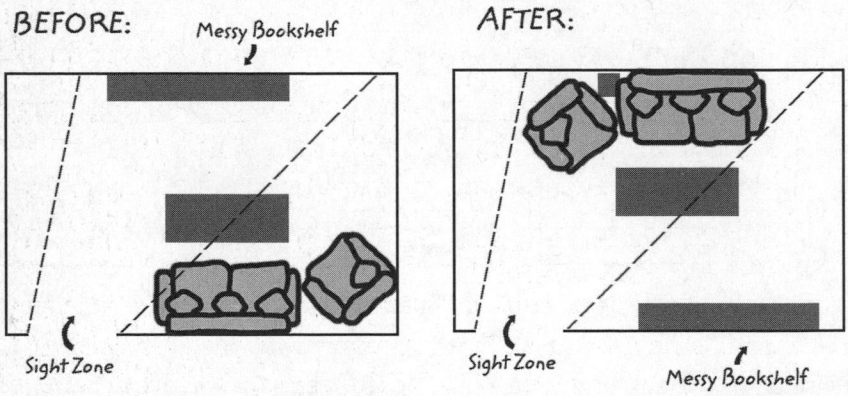

When you step into the room on the left, the first thing you see is the bookcase because it is against the wall opposite the door. If those shelves are messy, your impression of the entire room is that it's messy, even if it's not.

When you step into the room on the right, the bookcase has been placed next to the doorway you're in. To see those messy books, you have to step into the room and turn around. By that time, if the rest of the room is fairly neat, your brain will have already thought "neat." So this is how you should arrange this room to take advantage of the Sight Zone principle.

In Part 3 we'll go into more detail regarding using the Sight Zone principle throughout your home to reinforce that positive psychological experience of "neatness." For now, think about your family's messiest tendencies and where they manifest. Dresser tops, entertainment areas, and open shelving are some of the most likely culprits. As you work your way through the house, think in terms of locating these types of items out of the main line of sight.

You might also want to pay attention to some basic design principles, particularly the concept of establishing a focal point. Often our eyes wander throughout a room because there is no single spot that draws our eye. Give your family and guests satisfaction and ease by providing a focal point for every Sight Zone. Make sure those stay clean. For instance, a beautiful, lighted painting that hangs on the wall stays neat, but an attractive vividly colored toy shelf will tend to get messy. By all means, have vividly colored shelves if you want, just place them outside Sight Zones so you don't have to keep them clean at all times.

My Most Embarrassing Messy House Story

—A Nasty Surprise—

BY RITA P.

One time I brought my car to have it hand-detailed because it was so filthy and was starting to have an odor. When I went to pick it up, the man told me it wasn't ready yet. He brought me outside and showed me the problem.

Apparently some time back my toddler had dropped a bottle of milk, and it had rolled under the front passenger seat. In the time since, not only had the milk soured, but the bottle had leaked, drawing flies. I about died when I saw that the detailers had to remove the entire seat to clean under it because the whole floor was covered in maggots.

16

Record Future Improvements Needed

(CONVERT)

So if you have not been trustworthy in handling worldly wealth, who will trust you with true riches?

LUKE 16:11

Go back to area #1 and stand in the entryway. Start a fresh page in your notebook and title it "Repairs and Improvements." List any items in this area that would be far easier to keep clean if they were fixed or replaced. For example, you might write:

- permanent stain in carpet to right of door
- heater vent rusted on one side
- back wall needs fresh coat of paint
- plastic part of light fixture is dingy

As soon as possible, fix these problems yourself or ask your spouse to take care of them. Do as much as you can. You may not be able to afford new carpeting, but maybe a square can be pieced in or, at the very least, you can use scissors to snip off the pile until you have removed the worst part of the spot.

A House That Ceans Itself is a house that is in good repair. My friend Abby tells how she wasted valuable minutes every time she cleaned by trying to polish the brass switchplate beside her front door. Her hard work was to no avail. It always looked dull and marred. Killing time in a home repair center one day while waiting for her husband, she spotted an array of switchplates for sale. Much to her shock, she saw that she could replace the problem switchplate for a shiny new one for about $10. Considering the amount of time she'd wasted trying to clean something that was never going to get clean, she felt silly. It never crossed her mind that the item could be replaced so cheaply or easily.

Bathroom faucets often present the same problem. We lived for several years with a faucet that looked dirty and gunky all the time no matter what I did to clean it. I couldn't understand what I was doing wrong until my the plumber mentioned that the faucet appeared gunky because it had been sloppily caulked. Sure enough, I had been wasting my time on something that was never going to get any cleaner. Eventually we had that faucet replaced, but until then I never wasted another moment trying to get it clean.

My Most Embarrassing Messy House Story

—A Bathroom Surprise, Take 2—

BY STACI T.

I was distracted by many things, including homeschooling my children and working on church ministries. Who had time for deep-cleaning? I kept up on the basics—sweeping, picking up clutter, and such—but I let the serious scrubbing and mopping slide. One day I was in the bathroom, thinking it was probably time to break out the cleaners and get to it, when something small and dark-colored in the corner caught my eye.

I got down on my hands and knees to inspect more closely.

What I saw in this dark and damp corner horrified me. It was tiny and about the size of a raisin. I bent even closer and blinked to be sure. It was a mushroom! A mushroom growing in my bathroom.

We happened to be studying fungus in our homeschool science class, so I let the children photograph the specimen before eradicating it.

Then I cancelled school and spent the rest of the day going at every corner, nook, and cranny with bleach and a toothbrush. Life is still busy, and my house still isn't up to my mother-in-law's standards, but at least the only mushrooms are in cans in the pantry.

17

Take Steps Now for Ongoing Maintenance

(CONVERT)

Our people must learn to devote themselves to doing what is good, in order that they may provide for daily necessities and not live unproductive lives.

TITUS 3:14

Whatever you do, don't skim through this final step. Paying attention now will help guarantee your success in keeping each area neat and clean for good.

There are four elements to ongoing maintenance, each of which involves *preempting* mess. Before the mess even appears, you:

- anticipate "illegal parkers"
- anticipate trash
- anticipate purging
- anticipate dirt

Anticipate "Illegal Parkers"

Early in this book I told you to take pictures of each area. It's time for more pictures, but these are mental ones. Look around area #1. Note how it looks and what belongs here.

From now on the only items that should ever be in this area are the ones that are here right now. Think of it this way. Imagine this area is a private parking lot and you are the security guard. Your main job is to watch for any unfamiliar vehicles that try to park here. The moment you see one, you question the driver. If he doesn't have a parking permit, he's got to go.

Being a "home security guard" doesn't mean you are to constantly pick up after the other people as if you were a maid. It does mean you are going to become more aware of clutter and mess when it pops up so you can either get rid of it or call back the person who left it there and have him or her get rid of it. Explain to your family members about the parking lot analogy and let them know they are now security guards too.

In the future (at the risk of stretching my analogy a little thin), if a car keeps coming back and trying to park there, consider selling it a pass to the lot. In other words, if you find that some item or type of item keeps getting left here, consider whether it needs to be assigned a place within the area.

Learn to be diligent. Keep your eyes wide open. So much mess happens when we're looking the other way. Decide now to keep this area looking neat and clean. Keep illegal parkers out for good!

Anticipate Trash

This next step sounds so simple, but to the housekeeping impaired it's not. This is one of those things that is so important to keeping a clean home and yet frequently doesn't come to mind.

Ask yourself: If you were in this area and needed to throw something away, how far would you have to walk to do that? The correct answer is "no further than the very next room."

A house that cleans itself is a house where it is always easy and convenient to throw away trash. Ideally there should be a trash can in *every* room. But for smaller, more transitional areas such as an entryway, as long as there is a trash can in the next room that should suffice. Any further than that, and trash gets put down anywhere.

Make sure the trash cans in your main areas of trash accumulation—the kitchen, bathroom, and dressing area—are large enough to handle the job, convenient to get to, and simple to use.

Some people are worse about this than others. Ginger has a particular problem tossing out the packaging that comes with the things she buys. If she comes home with a new tube of lipstick, chances are the cardboard backing and the clear plastic cover will be torn away and left on some surface as she blithely heads to the nearest mirror to try out the new color. She also forgets to throw away the cellophane and stickers she tears from new CDs, the boxes from packages that come in the mail, and even the containers that get emptied of food as she cooks. Ginger is not a slob; she's just not likely to stop what she's doing to seek out a trash can. Needless to say, it doesn't take long for Ginger's house to get cluttered with things that belong in the trash.

As you work your way through your Flow Plan, make sure there is at least one trash can in every room, with only a few exceptions for the smallest transitional rooms. Furthermore, *make sure the trash cans in your main areas of trash accumulation—the kitchen, bathroom, and dressing area—are large enough to handle the job, convenient to get to, and simple to use.* For example, some people keep their kitchen trash in a can under the sink. This totally wouldn't work for me because if I have to open a door *before* I can toss something, I hesitate, set that trash on the counter, and decide to do it later—especially if I'm in the middle of cooking.

For the housekeeping impaired, throwing away trash should only require a single motion. (I admit, I do have a lidded can in my kitchen, but that lid is lifted by a foot pedal, which only counts as a half-motion.) If avoiding a multistep trash process sounds absurd to you, count yourself lucky that this isn't one of your impairments. If you find that someone in your family has trouble getting trash all the way to the trash can, consider simplifying your process. Pull the can out of the cabinet or get rid of the lid and see if the issue clears up.

Anticipate Purging

Don't think for a moment that the purge you're doing as you CONVERT your house is a one-time thing. Purging is an ongoing, cyclical action. Think about how often new possessions get brought into your home. To prevent a build-up of clutter, older and unwanted items should be going back out in the same quantity. Even if you grasp this thought in principle, the doing often seems more complicated.

Let's say you have a pair of jeans that shrunk in the dryer. You can't wear them anymore, but they're too good to throw away. In a messy house, you would probably set those jeans aside, intending to donate them eventually. Soon, however, the jeans are lost in the clutter or, worse, get accidentally integrated back into the closet. Fortunately there is a solution to this problem: Set up one or two permanent "Charity Buckets" in your home. Anytime you run across an item you don't want or need, place that item in the nearest Charity Bucket (which is really nothing more than a clean, lidded trash can lined with a plastic bag). Items may accumulate quickly or slowly, but the key to making the system work is the follow-through: When the bucket gets full, you simply pull out the plastic bag filled with your donations, tie it off, and get it to its final destination.

Most homes only need one or two Charity Buckets. That's how many we have: the Upstairs Charity Bucket (UCB), which we keep on the floor of the linen closet, and the Downstairs Charity Bucket (DCB), which we keep just inside the interior door to the garage. Our UCB is the size of a tall kitchen can, but our DCB is much bigger, the size of an outdoor can. That way we can purge items large and small with ease. Because we itemize our contributions for tax purposes, we have a sheet of paper and pencil nearby so as a person deposits an item he or she can list it and its value. If you need to do this too, one idea is to hang a clipboard with paper and a pencil on a nearby wall or directly to the container.

Because you will be doing so much purging in the coming weeks and/or months, you may not want to set up your permanent Charity Bucket(s) just yet. But after your home has been fully converted into a House That Cleans Itself, take those two cans that you bought for sorting purposes, clean them out, and designate them as your Charity Buckets. Place them somewhere out of the way but convenient, like in a centrally located cabinet or closet. Once that's done, challenge your entire family to see how quickly they can fill them up.

Anticipate Dirt

It's time now to turn your attention to the dirt and grime of daily living. Houses get dirty and they need cleaning. That's a fact of life. From the mud we track in to the skin we slough off, we humans can't escape the basic truth that life is messy. If you are housekeeping impaired, chances are that you think of cleaning as an isolated event you do periodically in an all-or-nothing fashion.

In fact, cleaning is not like that at all. It's not something you do once a week for two hours or once every two weeks for five. In a House That Cleans Itself, *cleaning is an activity that must be integrated into your everyday life* just like brushing your teeth or taking your medicine. Cleaning may not be tons of fun, but it doesn't have to be all that big of a deal either. In many ways, the HTCI plan is about changing your house rather than your behavior, but in this area, your behavior must change as well.

Much of my personal housekeeping battle came to an end when I finally surrendered my all-or-nothing tendency and decided I didn't want to be that way anymore. I reframed my concept of what "cleaning" means and set up three different Stations to reflect this new way of thinking:

- Quick Cleaning—to be used frequently to wipe up small messes, such as crumbs, smears, and fingerprints

- Intermediate Cleaning—also to be used frequently to clean up small messes that require larger tools that can't be duplicated in every room, such as a rechargeable vacuum and an instant mop
- Deep Cleaning—to be used for the regular, more involved cleaning that every house requires on a periodic basis

Let's assemble these Stations. In the next chapter, we'll explore the best ways to use them to keep everything clean.

Quick Clean Stations

A Quick Clean Station is exactly what the name implies. It is a collection of cleaning products and supplies gathered together in a single container and placed in a convenient location so you can quickly and easily get rid of messes in that location. Almost every one of the rooms in your house should have its own Quick Clean Station. In many cases the station will consist of nothing more than a pack of disposable wipes.

Can you imagine what would happen if you put an assortment of disposable wipes in nearly every room of your house? Do you think you might be more likely to give the dirty bathroom counter a swipe if all you had to do was reach into the medicine cabinet and pull out a wipe? How easy it is to clean the front window when a pack of window-cleaning wipes is tucked in the nearest drawer! To the housekeeping impaired, disposable wipes can be one of the most useful tools you will ever have at your fingertips. Buy them and use them. They are wonderful.

Quick Clean Stations should contain wipes that are appropriate for each surface in that room. For example, if you have a ceramic, glass, or porcelain cooktop, you should buy a bottle of cleaner for big clean-ups and also a can of stove-top wipes for faster jobs. The wipes I prefer are smooth on one side and safely abrasive on the other, which makes them handy for scrubbing burned-on messes without harming the finish. In the bathroom you might have antibacterial wipes for the counter, sink, toilet, and bath, and glass wipes for the mirror and window. For the living room, you may include electronic wipes for the stereo components and dusting wipes for wood furniture. (Though you should avoid using any chemicals on your finest wood.) If you don't have room for all of these canisters, buy them in flat packages.

Intermediate Level Cleaning Tools

Some of the messes you come across are going to require bigger tools, such as a mop or vacuum cleaner, and you can't have one of these in every room. You can, however, have these intermediate level cleaning tools for each of the major sections of your home. You might have one set upstairs and one set downstairs. Your intermediate level tools include:

- a rechargeable, battery-operated vacuum cleaner, such as a Shark
- an automatic mop, such as a Swiffer WetJet
- an extendable ostrich-feather duster

Frankly I never realized how far technology had come on rechargeable vacuum cleaners until I saw one being used at my church—and it's a big church. I asked the maintenance staff about it and got such an enthusiastic response that I went out and bought one for myself. Sure enough, it cleans almost as well as my full-size, heavy-duty vacuum cleaner, but it has no cord to get in the way and weighs practically nothing. The main trade-off, at least on the model I bought, is that the dirt-collecting tank is so small it has to be dumped often. The charge holds for about 45 minutes worth of vacuuming.

By making these cleaning tools convenient to the part of the house you're in, you are much more likely to grab and use them when you spot a mess. More importantly, your kids will too, although they may need to be reminded now and then.

Deep Cleaning Station

Somewhere in your home you must establish a place for all those other cleaning tools (including the heavy-duty versions of the intermediate level tools). From silver polish to oven cleaner, paper towels to rubber gloves, the items you need to get your house clean should be accessible, organized, and uncluttered. Did you know that cleaners can cause clutter? Take a look in your cleaning closet. Toss all out-of-date items as well as any that you never use. Just because that expanding dryer-lint-hose-wiper was a good idea when you bought it doesn't mean you'll ever get around to using it again. Does it really deserve to take up three square feet of prime closet space?

Once you have purged all but the essentials from your Deep Cleaning Station, look at what's left. Are any important tools or products missing? Think in terms of supplies for the following:

- *general surfaces* (spray cleaners, sponges, magic eraser, and rags)
- *specialized surfaces* (wood polish and oven cleaner)
- *floors* (broom, mop and extra mop heads, bucket, floor cleaner, and vacuum cleaner with extra attachments and bags)
- *trash* (trash bags and string for recycling newspapers)

How you organize your cleaners depends on the space you are working with. I keep my cleaners inside a closet on a metal shelving unit. My friend Sue has most of hers hanging from hooks in a pegboard in her laundry room. Whatever system you use, make sure your Deep Cleaning Station has everything you really need and nothing you don't.

Apply What You've Learned

Set up the quick clean station for area #1 now. If possible, acquire and establish the intermediate level tools for this part of your house as well. (For the Deep Cleaning Station, you may need to wait until you have purged and cleared the area you intend to use.)

If you recall, one of the cleaning problems in area #1 was that dirt and fingerprints were waiting until cleaning day to get cleared away. As you can see, now that you have glass-cleaning wipes stashed somewhere in the area, it is quick and easy to grab one and make short work of those fingerprints. As for the dirt on the floor, help isn't too far away either. With the battery-charged vacuum and the automatic mop, you can make short work of that as well.

In Part 3 we'll discuss choosing the right deep-cleaning plan for your family. But with these quick and intermediate level tools now at your fingertips day to day, the deep cleaning in your house will go more smoothly and take far less time.

My Most Embarrassing Messy House Story

—Microwave Madness—

BY GINGER S.

I once moved aside a borrowed microwave that my husband and I had been using for several months to put in its place one that had been given to us as a Christmas present. In all the confusion, I forgot to clean the inside of the borrowed one, and it got shoved into the garage.

Months later the friend who loaned the microwave to us was at our home for a party. My husband said, "Oh, we can give you back that microwave now." He went to the garage and brought the oven into the party. Before I could react, he popped open the door in front of everyone.

The microwave looked and smelled like something from my worst nightmare. Actually, that whole experience *was* my worst nightmare—except it really happened!

18

The Checklist

My son, preserve sound judgment and discernment,
do not let them out of your sight;
they will be life for you, an ornament to grace your neck.
Then you will go on your way in safety, and your foot will not
stumble; when you lie down, you will not be afraid;
when you lie down, your sleep will be sweet.

PROVERBS 3:21 24

Now that the conversion of area #1 on your Flow Plan is complete, let's review what you've accomplished. Have you:

1. *Changed the areas to fit the behavior?*
   Yes, by creating more convenient places to store the items that go in and out.
2. *Changed the behavior to fit the areas, but only after you've changed the areas as much as possible?*
   Yes, by assigning a new, more convenient home to the items that can't fit in the entryway.
3. *Controlled your "expected messy areas" and "Sight Zones"?*
   Yes, by putting the launch pad bulletin board inside a cabinet with a door and adjusting the Sight Zone to limit the view from the front door.
4. *Thought "Up and Away?"*
   Take a look around to make sure. Is there anything in

this entryway that can be mounted on a wall rather than placed on a surface? Kept in a closet or cabinet rather than left out in plain sight? Force yourself to see this space in its entirety, just like you did from the top of the step stool. Does it look uncluttered and neat?

5. *Thought like a housecleaning service?*
   Only you can answer that. How hard was it to purge the clutter you ran across in this area? Are you able to see your home for what it is and understand what it is not?

6. *Emphasized simplicity?*
   Yes, by purging every speck of clutter from this room that you could. But what about the items that remain? Are they easy to maintain? Have you made clean-friendly choices with regard to design, color, and decoration? How about the *purpose* of this space? Has that been simplified and/or clarified as well?

7. *Engineered convenience?*
   Yes, by setting up a launching pad that accommodates every household, and by moving the homes of the items that come in the house closer to the door.

8. *Utilized the power of beauty?*
   Is the space merely utilitarian or is it aesthetically pleasing as well? Save any major redecorating projects until after the full conversion (your hands are full enough already!), but if a coat of paint or a new houseplant will perk up this area and make your family members more likely to keep it clean, consider making those changes now.

9. *Camouflaged wherever possible?*
   Are you using the art of camouflage to its full effect in this room? Take one more look at your choices in colors and textures. If you can make any changes to more durable and dirt-hiding options, do that now.

10. *Done everything with an eye toward maintenance?*
    Yes, by making sure there is a convenient trash can in the

next room, by setting up a convenient Charity Bucket, by creating a Quick Clean Station, and by setting up intermediate level tools nearby.

Now that area #1 is finished, most of the principles and steps of the House That Cleans Itself System should be clear in your mind. Reward yourself for a job well done so far!

Okay, now it's time to move to Part 3 of this book—and to the rest of your house, area by area, until you have converted every single one. Get out your Flow Plan and move on to area #2.

You got ready. You got set. Now...go!

My Most Embarrassing Messy House Moment

—An Ice Cube Surprise—

BY NELLIE K.

For my sixteenth birthday my mother decided to go all out and cook a fancy sit-down dinner for me and seven of my closest friends. The night of the celebration the dining room table looked elegant dressed with a lace tablecloth, crystal goblets, and fine china. About halfway through the meal one of my friends gasped: In her fancy goblet was a half-melted ice cube from which protruded a glob of previously chewed bubble gum...complete with teeth marks!

My mother was mortified beyond belief. She'd wanted to give me a birthday I would never forget, but this wasn't exactly what she had in mind.

That was many years ago, but I've never forgotten it—and I still don't know how a fully chewed piece of gum got frozen into an ice cube.

Part 3

Go!

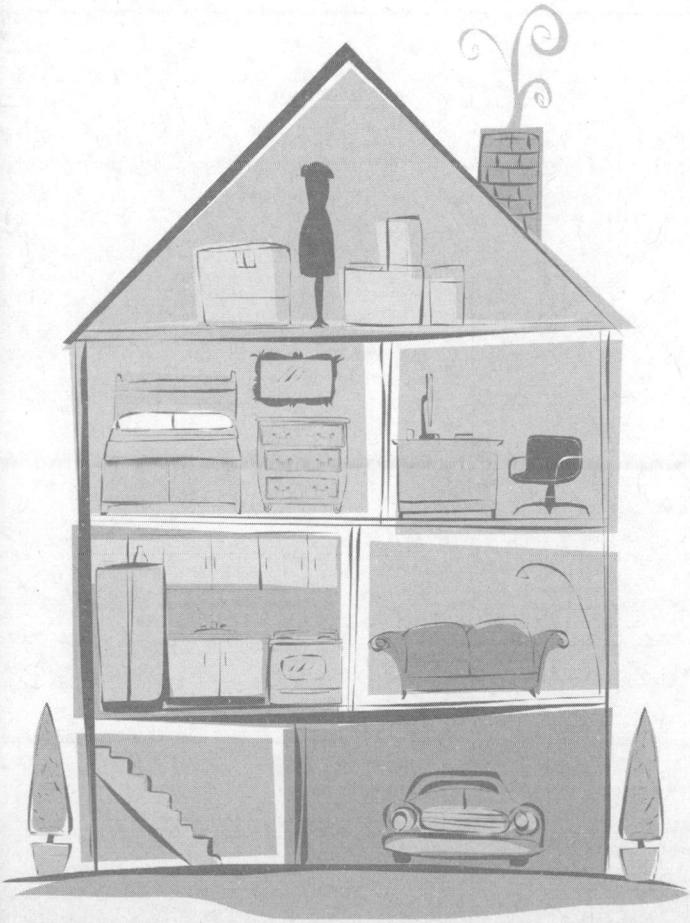

19

Work Your Way Through the House

Whatever you do, work at it with all your heart, as working for the Lord, not for men, since you know that you will receive an inheritance from the Lord as a reward. It is the Lord Christ you are serving.

COLOSSIANS 3:23-24

It is now time to pull out your Flow Chart and move to area #2 on your list. Bring along the tools you used in area #1, including your notebook, a pen or pencil, the two trash cans and bags, the laundry basket, the cardboard boxes, a sorting Station if you are using one, a marker, a labelmaker or labels, a measuring tape, a blanket or quilt, and cleaning supplies.

You are now going to start back at the letter "C" in the CONVERT plan (see chapter 11) for this next area and repeat the steps you followed in area #1, the entryway. For the sake of clarity, I'll reiterate these steps.

Clear out the clutter. Start by attacking the visible items on counters and tables and then moving into drawers, containers, cabinets, and closets. Purge as much as you can, giving away or throwing away. Remember to place in the laundry basket all items that don't belong in this room. After the clutter has been completely cleared from this entire area, move out the bags of donations and trash, put your sorting cans and boxes into the next area on your schedule, drape the blanket over them, and then return to this area.

Open up and clean. Use your deep-cleaning tools for vacuuming, dusting, wiping, and mopping.

Neaten, organize, and solve problem spots. Using your notebook, review the list you made of messes in this room and their root causes. Use creative problem solving to eliminate those causes. (The next part of this chapter includes a list of many types of rooms, the typical problems you might find in them, and some suggestions for solutions.)

Verify and set up Stations as needed. Turn to the part of your notebook where you listed the Stations you want to implement in your home. Decide if any of those Stations will be located in this room. If so, set them up. Remember that if you need to buy containers, measure the space where the container will go and determine how much it needs to hold.

Examine Sight Zones. Now that the room has been purged, cleaned, neatened, and problem-solved, stand in the doorway and make sure the Sight Zone is neat and attractive and that it has a focal point. Fix any problems you notice.

Record future improvements needed. In your notebook make a list of any maintenance issues that need to be addressed in this area, as well as any larger changes you want to make to this space in the future.

Take steps now for ongoing maintenance. Make a mental note of how this room looks now and what items belong in this space. Verify that there is a trash can in this room or next door. Set up a small Quick Clean Station for this room.

Area #2 is now converted into the House That Cleans Itself System! You can move along to area #3 and repeat the CONVERT steps for that area. Continue to do this in every area on your Flow Chart until your house and yard are complete.

Tips for Your Home's Interior and Exterior

- Use the physical space in your home to limit what you

bring into it. That means you can own no more clothes than the closet can hold, no more books than the bookshelf can hold, and so forth.

- Invest in a digital labelmaker to help with sorting and keep your storage areas neat. Digital labelmakers are available in a variety of sizes, shapes, and prices. Though they start at about $30, they're worth every penny, especially if you're making a concerted effort to get organized. Check your local office supply or discount store to see the choices that are available. (When you get one, be sure to buy batteries for it, along with a few extra rolls of label tape to have on hand.) Using your new labelmaker is as simple as typing the words you need on a small keyboard, pressing the print button, and watching the label shoot out of the machine.
- Talk to your plumber or local water utility about whether there's any need for installing a water treatment system in your home. If you have unusually hard water, for example, a softener can increase the life of your washing machine and decrease the staining in your tubs and sinks.
- Change the filter on your central air conditioner regularly. A clean filter can prevent the spread of dust and improve the air quality in your home.
- Choose furniture and fixtures with an eye toward uniformity and simplicity. The more elaborate the ornamentation, the more dusting will be required to keep it clean.
- If you have pets, camouflage your home with them in mind. For example, don't put dark carpeting in a house that has dogs with light-colored fur.
- If you are upgrading your windows or doors, check the latest low-maintenance features on the market. Two of my favorites include blinds encased inside the glass

(no more dusting miniblinds!) and top-hung sliding glass doors so dirt doesn't collect in a track below. Even lower-cost windows are now coming standard with easy-to-clean features such as a tilt-in capability.

- The technology has already been achieved for self-cleaning glass, though you may have to do a bit of hunting to find a manufacturer you can afford. A miracle of nanotechnology, these windows are coated in titanium dioxide, which works with the sun and the rain to do the cleaning for you. (The sun's ultraviolet light reacts with titanium dioxide to break down the organic chemicals in dirt. The rain produces a sheeting action that washes away the larger particles. Amazing!)

  In the not-too-distant future, scientists expect to release other products that utilize a similar technology, such as self-cleaning house paint.

- If you've worked your way through the book this far, you already have the best self-cleaning tool of all: You have a house that cleans itself!

Area by Area Problems and Solutions

To help your conversion process, I've included a list of problems that can crop up all around your home, along with some HTCI-type solutions.

Exterior Front

Problem: There are green patches on the roof and walls.

Try this: If algae or moss tends to grow in certain areas of your roof or walls, trim back nearby greenery that may be preventing the sunlight from reaching those areas. You'll still have to get the algae off this time, but with more direct sunlight from now on the green may not return or will return more slowly.

Sometimes moss will also grow upward from a clogged rain gutter if the clog has been sitting long enough. Clear out your gutters and install gutter guards so they never again get clogged with sticks, leaves, and sediment, which leads to green growing things.

Problem: Outside trash cans are too visible, ruining the look of the house.

Try this: Do your trash cans have a "place"? If not, establish one in a convenient but discreet location, maybe behind a fence or a lattice wall. If the cans have a place but it's not getting used, determine the reasons why and fix them.

At Joanie's house the trash cans belonged around the side, behind a tall bush, but her teenage son never got them all the way there. Instead, he usually dragged them up the driveway and left them in plain sight. Looking more closely at the situation, Joanie realized that the problem was twofold: the short path from the driveway to behind the bush tended to get muddy, and it was also dark at night, making it difficult to maneuver. By creating a gravel walkway for the cans and installing a motion detector light at that corner of the house, Joanie eliminated the trash can problem.

Problem: Toys are left scattered in the yard.

Try this: Place an all-weather storage chest or bench in a convenient place outside—on the porch or near the garage—so that it's easier for your kids to put their outside toys away.

Problem: Flower beds are full of weeds because it's too much trouble to bend over and pull them out.

Try this: Convert those ground-level beds into waist-high planters. You'll still have to deal with the weeds, but you won't have to bend over to do so.

Also, to eliminate most weeds take advantage of plastic sheeting sold in garden supply stores. The sheeting goes under your mulch so it can't be seen and stops most weeds before they start.

Entryway—Dirt on Dirt

Problem: Dirt is continuously tracked into the home.

Try this: Always have two welcome mats, one outside with a rough texture to take off the heavy-duty grime, and one inside, perhaps a washable floor rug, for a secondary measure. Make sure each of these rugs is as big as your space can accommodate without detracting from the décor. The more times a shoe strikes a mat while walking, the more dirt will come off that shoe before it can be tracked into the rest of the house.

In this era of deep-tread sneakers, welcome mats are more overworked than ever before. If the dirt coming into your home continues to be a problem, consider taking these extra steps:

- Add a roughly-textured boot scraper near the door. (My neighbor has a cute one that looks like a porcupine.)
- Put an open shoe rack or basket just inside the door, and train friends and family to remove their shoes as soon as they come inside. To make them more likely to use it, place a bench or chair nearby so they have somewhere to sit as they take off their shoes. You might also consider providing slippers, flip-flops, and other indoor-only shoes for the ones who don't want to go barefoot.

Living Room/Den/Family Room

Problem: The lamp shades look dirty.

Try this: Dust them with a lint roller, the kind that has a peel-and-stick surface.

Problem: Curio shelves and book shelves are always dusty.

Try this: Replace open shelving with glass-fronted cabinets. Dust will still accumulate on the shelves but much more slowly, turning a weekly dusting chore into one that only needs to be done every few months.

Problem: Collection of curios is taking over room.

Try this: Consider these simple guidelines for collecting:

1. It's okay to stop. Collections can be finite. There is no "collection rule book" that says you must continue to acquire more items.
2. It's okay to get rid of it. As we age, we lose interest in different hobbies. Just because something was important to you once doesn't mean you "owe" it anything now. Objects do not have feelings!
3. It's okay to rotate it. If you love your collection, but it takes up too much space, let your items take turns in the spotlight. Put the excess in a storage container, and rotate the items once or twice a year.

Problem: The coats are always accumulating on the coat rack and sometimes sit there long after the season is over.

Try this: First, decide whether coats have a place all together, such as a coat closet, or if they will be divided into the individual users' closets, like other clothing. Then find out if your dry cleaner has a discount day (such as Tuesdays). With that in mind, pick an appropriate date on your calendar (even if it's months away) and write down an appointment with yourself to take the coats to the cleaners. Seeing that appointment will also remind you to wash the coats and jackets that are machine-washable. Put all the clean coats wherever they belong in the off-season.

Problem: We are drowning in magazines and newspapers.

Try this: Embrace this truth, one that is utterly necessary in this age of information overload: Just because something is printed and distributed and ends up your home doesn't mean you have to read it—even if you paid for it. If you have too many magazines and newspapers, put them in the recycling bin or throw them away. Better yet, find someplace that might want them, such as retirement homes, clinics, or athletic clubs. Make a point of passing along last month's issue as soon as the new one comes out.

Think time. Is reading month-old news or yet another retread of the same idea worth the trade-off of time? If you have a backlog of reading material, you're allowing too many of these items into your home in the first place. Allow your subscriptions to run out and don't renew. Instead, when you get eager for something to read, check your local library, which may have a wide selections of magazine available for checkout.

Work, Weather, and Kids

Problem: The house falls apart on the days when there's no school, such as on snow days and lesser holidays. The normal routine is disrupted.

Try this: Anticipate messes like these by preempting the day off with temporary stations.

Fun Stations: Set up various activities in different places in the house, such as a jigsaw puzzle waiting to be assembled on the dining table, a painting set ready to use in the playroom, and a selection of board games ready to play on the coffee table. Kids are more likely to make a mess if they're bored and have nothing to do.

Food and Beverage Station: Put out healthful snacks along with a Hot Chocolate Station (mugs, cocoa powder, water, spoons, marshmallows).

Serve lunch as a picnic on the floor of the living room using disposable plates and cups on a big tablecloth or sheet. When the meal is finished, toss the disposable items in the trash. Gather up the sheet, shake the crumbs out the back door, and put the sheet in the washer.

"Contained" Active-Play Stations: Keep the kids from running wild all over the house by creating special spaces or activities for them:

- Put a big sheet over a card table to create a tent.
- Wire your camcorder directly into the VCR, turn it on, and

place it on top of the television, facing the room. When the kids turn on the TV, they will see themselves on the screen. (Even toddlers love jumping up and down while watching themselves do the same thing on television.)

- Place masking tape over the bathtub faucets as a reminder not to turn them, and then fill the tub with cozy blankets and a stack of books.
- Set up a karaoke area for preteens with a microphone, CD player, and karaoke CDs.

Preserve the peace: When kids are bored, they'll wander everywhere, even when there's no reason to do so. If there are rooms in the house that are perfectly clean and don't need to be used for any reason, shut the doors and run packing tape across the doorways at eye level to serve as a reminder not to open. Or you can block the doorways with chairs. Tell your kids these rooms are off limits for the day.

Set up a temporary Gear Removal Station: Place several beach towels at each entrance, and move a piece of furniture, such as a bench or light table, several feet inside of the door, blocking the way just enough to serve as a reminder that all who enter should strip off snow or rain gear before coming any further. Tell them to use the beach towels to dry up the ice and snow that falls from their outerwear as they take it off. If possible, place a clothes-drying rack or ad-hoc clothesline with clothespins nearby for hanging damp items.

Give yourself a break: Ever want to stop the world and get off? That's what days like these are for! Forget the mess and hang with the kids. Spend some unexpected time with your spouse too. Settle the kids in front of a movie, pull on your own snow gear, and take a quiet stroll together through the winter wonderland outside. You can always clean tomorrow.

Problem: My kids won't leave me alone so I can clean.

Try this: If your kids like toy-related pretend play, such as Barbies or Hot Wheels, then preempt a busy day at home for you by starting them off with a fun distraction that can last for hours. The night before, after they are asleep, set up a "scene" in their play area, such as a dollhouse neighborhood or a toy car road adventure. Incorporate some of their toys, along with an imaginative use of some ordinary household items such as empty boxes for tunnels or folded washcloths for doll beds. Run a long string through the handle of a basket, and tie the string onto knobs or handles so that it stretches the length of the room about two feet off of the floor. Put a doll or car inside the basket.

When the kids wake up, let them discover this prestaged wonderland. Chances are they will be so enchanted that they'll jump right in and start adding to the display and playing. When my girls were little, as long as I didn't do it too often, this was my best secret weapon. They would stay busy for hours in one room.

Oh yes—tell them the basket is a tram to transport the dolls or cars from one end of the room to the other. This alone will use up an enormous amount of time as they upload and offload that basket in a series of exciting storylines that require such an amazing transportation device. Sometimes, kids are so easy to distract.

Ditch This Ought

I ought to read the newspaper every day.

Says who?

Don't do it if it doesn't work for you!

Problem: My kids won't put away video games after they play them or DVDs after they watch them.

Try this: Ask them why not. Sometimes children aren't being lazy or inconsiderate as much as they are being subconsciously avoidant or even totally unaware. Maybe the rack is stuffed so full or the slots are so narrow that the DVD shelf is hard to use. Maybe the basket for the video games is so high they have to stand up to use it, something they aren't likely to do when they're plopped comfortably on the floor.

Rather than nagging at them to change their behavior, approach the matter like investigative teammates solving a problem together. Sit down on the floor right where the mess usually happens and ask your kids to think about why they continue to do this behavior even though you have told them not to. Explain the House That Cleans Itself approach for situations like these and ask them what they think could be done to make putting these items away easier and more instinctive. Let them take ownership for the solution that you agree on together and "prove" to you their idea will work.

They may also need to work on their self-discipline, but it never hurts to change the house first and then work on the behavior.

Kitchen

Problem: My glass cooktop keeps getting scorch marks.

Try this: Every time you cook, keep a wet washcloth or hand towel nearby. Though you're not supposed to clean the cooktop when the surface is hot, if your pot boils over, wipe away the spill immediately. Be careful not to burn yourself! Do any further cleaning once the cooktop has cooled.

Problem: My kitchen looks messy even when it's not.

Try this: That's probably because too many items have their "place" right on your countertop. To solve this problem, do an experiment. Take every single thing from your kitchen counters that isn't hooked on and put it all in an out-of-the-way, nearby place. For the next week, if you need an item such as a toaster or a coffee maker, bring it back into the kitchen, use it, and leave it there. At the end of the week, whatever didn't make its way back to the kitchen doesn't belong on the kitchen counter. Assign these items new homes. Why should you look every day at a Crock-Pot you're only going to use once every two weeks or a breadmaker you're only going to use once a month? Everything that's not used on a nearly daily basis should be tucked out of sight.

While you're at it, move the hanging pot holders to a drawer, the artwork on the fridge to a bulletin board, and the stuff that's on top of the fridge to a cabinet. Kitchens start looking messy when we stop "seeing" them. Look at yours with a new eye, and remove anything that doesn't absolutely need to be in sight.

Problem: My sink is always dirty, even when there aren't dishes in it.

Try this: If you tend to clean the dishes and the counters but forget to clean the sink, reframe your thinking. Tell yourself that the last dirty "dish" you have to clean *is* the sink. I know it sounds dumb, but once I started thinking this way, sink clean-up became the final, automatic step in my dishwashing routine.

Problem: Food is getting lost in the depths of the fridge.

Try this: Measure your shelf and buy a lazy Susan big enough to fit with only an inch or so to spare at the sides. Food is less likely to disappear because you can spin the lazy Susan to find what you need.

Ditch This Ought

Every kitchen needs a spice rack.

Says who?

Don't do it if it doesn't work for you!

Problem: My spices are always going out of date before I finish them.

Try this: Stop buying so many spices. Somewhere, some time, someone planted the idea in our heads that cooks need spice racks and that those spice racks must be filled with every available spice. If you keep so many spices around because you use a lot of them when you cook, then ignore this advice. But if you keep so many spices around because that's what other people do, it's time to simplify. Some of the best cooks I know use only four spices: salt, pepper, garlic, and cinnamon. Consider whether you could lessen your spice load as well.

Problem: I'm spending too much time washing dishes or loading them into the dishwasher.

Try this: Surely someone has done the mathematical equation that tells how much time you add to the cleaning of a dish for every hour you allow that dish to sit dirty. I was always one of those people who could let dirty dishes wait a while (okay, sometimes a great while), but the best catalyst for change I found is this time wasted/time lost paradox. As food hardens and sets, the job gets harder. If you feel like you spend too much time doing dishes, it may be because you are waiting too long to do them.

If that's not the case, you still have two possibilities for cutting down this particular workload. Either delegate that chore to someone else in the family or integrate some disposable paper products into your routine. For example, pizza should always be eaten using paper plates. (You'll want to balance this need for convenience with your desire to be a good steward of the earth's resources.)

Problem: When I get home from the grocery store, I'm too tired to put everything away. I end up with boxes and cans cluttering the counters.

Try this: Again, delegation can be a big help here. The chore of "putting away the groceries" could go on the list of any child who is big enough to reach the cabinets.

If you have no one to delegate to, or if you like to put the groceries away yourself because that reminds you of what you bought, consider the following possibilities:

- Is your pantry too messy or too full? Sometimes we avoid this task because we know the stuff won't all fit or we realize that it's only going to get lost in there. If this is your situation, clear out that pantry, decide on categories, label the shelves, and get that place organized.
- Maybe your pantry is *too* organized? If you have a tendency to over-categorize, then putting away the groceries can be such a mental challenge that you avoid it entirely. Take a look at your pantry and see if this is the case. If it is, remove those labels and try again with more general categories, such as 3 kinds of cans (Soup, Vegetables, and Other) instead of 12.
- If neither of these issues is your problem, as a last ditch effort establish a "Temp Zone" for things that come into your house in plastic bags. Keep a big basket or an area of cabinet space clear for just this purpose. Don't forget to put away fridge and freezer items first, of course, but then put everything else in the Temp Zone and set a limit on how long they can remain there before you come back and put them where they really belong. This is an especially good solution for you if you suffer from some fatigue-related disorder. This way you avoid overtaxing your body while also keeping your house clean.

Problem: I hate using a dustpan so I avoid sweeping the kitchen floor until I absolutely have to.

Try this: Consider buying an "automatic dust pan," also known as a freestanding, central vacuum unit, Basically this is a sucking machine with a motion detector. The one I have cost about $50, is the size and shape of a computer hard drive, and sits permanently in the corner of my kitchen near a plug. Every time I sweep, I end by sweeping the pile under the unit. Sensing the motion of the broom, the machine kicks on and sucks the dirt into a tank. The only other effort required is to pull off the easily removable tank and dump the contents into the trash about once a month.

Some people don't "get" this product, and they look at me like I'm crazy when I show it to them. Others, however, understand immediately, and they get a gleam in their eye at the very thought. If the idea of this product appeals to you, try one. Truly, it's one of my favorite tools in the whole house.

Problem: My refrigerator always looks sloppy because it's covered with magnets and papers.

Try this: The fridge seems like a good place to hang up reminders because it is so centrally located and frequently visited. But those are also the two main reasons you should avoid the temptation to do this.

Place a bulletin board nearby instead, preferably on the inside of a door or cabinet so that you can see it whenever you want but can hide it when you want to neaten the room.

Problem: We're thinking about renovating the kitchen. Are there any House That Cleans Itself guidelines?

Try this: Yes, in fact I kept this very question in mind the whole time I was going through my own renovation process.

Cabinet doors. Because you want the room to be beautiful, you'll probably choose the door style based more on décor and taste than practicality. Bear in mind though, that the more angles and lines and ridges and grooves your cabinets have, the harder you will have to work to keep them clean. When they are shiny and new, that might not seem so bad, but considering your kitchen may last for 20 years, that can be a lot of extra cleaning time. Since the more complicated designs usually cost more, going for a simpler option will save you money as well.

Cabinet finish. Choose a wood finish that is neither too light nor too dark. Dirt hides better somewhere in the middle.

Cabinet configuration. Before you meet with a kitchen expert, sit down by yourself in your kitchen and brainstorm about the most efficient uses for your space. Think about your cooking routine and the tools you regularly employ. Some people cook with every container, utensil, pot, and pan in the house as they go. Others can whip up a delicious meal with nothing but a big bowl, one pan, and a spoon. Wherever you fall on that spectrum, decide not to keep any superfluous kitchen tools. If you rarely have more than one burner going at a time, why do you need eight pots?

Once you have a better idea of what a working kitchen for your style of cooking should include, you're ready to go to a kitchen designer and find out about the cool options available for cabinets these days.

Cabinet options. Consider drawers rather than cabinets (I now have two drawers that are each more than a foot deep, perfect for holding my pots and Crock-Pot); spinning corner units; multilayered pantries; wide, shallow drawers for cooking utensils; fold out "scrubby holders" on the front of the sink cabinet, and more. Use your imagination and have fun.

Countertop. Natural stone such as granite and quartz are the most durable, show the least amount of crumbs and dirt, offer some natural antibacterial properties, and are the easiest to keep clean and looking new. If you prefer a different surface, or your budget doesn't include real stone, there are many other alternatives, each with its own plusses and minuses. Talk to your kitchen designer before you decide.

Sink and faucet. Consider having your sink and faucet undermounted. Because that eliminates the "lip," cleaning is much easier. For my new kitchen, I took a chance on a black granite undermount sink, and I can't say enough good things about it. I was afraid the black would show mess, but because the stone is more of a sparkly dark gray than black, everything blends in. When the sink is clean and dry, it looks especially beautiful. Beauty being a great motivator, I try to keep it that way whenever I can. Not realizing it, I also chose a sink that was deeper than the one we had before, and that has been a great mess-buster. Not only is there less water splashed on the counter, but a few dirty dishes can sit in the bottom of the sink and not be visible from the Sight Zone.

Floor. If you're not sure what kind of flooring you want for your kitchen, get samples so you can conduct a House That Cleans Itself experiment. Place the samples on the floor in the dirtiest areas of the kitchen (in front of the sink, the stove, and the fridge). Ignore them for a week. At the end of the week, see which sample is doing the best job of hiding the dirt that has accumulated. Let that be your deciding factor.

Appliances. Think fingerprints, fingerprints, fingerprints. As you are choosing appliances for your kitchen, place your hand flatly against the outside surface. Remove your hand and study the effect from several angles, close and far. Choose the type of finish that hid your handprint best.

Small appliances. Think up and away. Almost all small appliances come in versions that can be mounted under your cabinets, including toasters, coffeemakers, and can openers. If you like to listen to music or watch television when you cook, get an undermount, flip down TV/DVD/CD/Radio unit, which usually costs from $100 on up.

Dining Room

Problem: I need a better way to sort my tablecloths and other linens.

Try this: Fold dinner napkins inside their matching tablecloths, and then sort tablecloths into piles based on their shape and size (small round, large round, square, oblong). Before you put them neatly away, ask yourself if you have more than you need. If so, purge the tablecloths you rarely use or don't really like.

Home Office

Problem: Wires are everywhere.

Try this: Give those wires some attention. First, label them at both ends to save time during setup. Second, neatly corral them by using twist ties to group them together. (Office supply stores also have various products to help you control messy cords.)

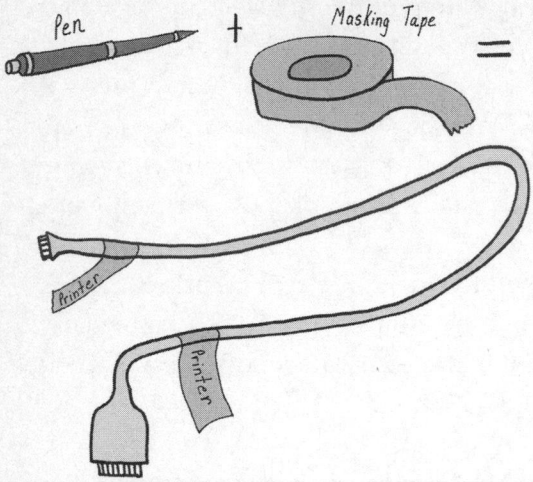

Problem: I have so many projects going at once that I need to leave them all out on the desk, but that ends up making a mess.

Try this: Consider this innovative solution that I came up with for my home office. Visit a restaurant supply store or check online for a baker's rack (also called a "jelly rack" or "donut rack").

I got this idea one time while standing in a Krispy Kreme shop, watching the donut-making process through the window. As donuts came off the conveyor belt, they were placed on a large plastic tray. Each time a tray was full, the attendant would carry it to the rack, slide it into place, and take out the next tray. Watching this, it struck me that I could handle the projects in my office somewhat the same way. Rather than using file folders (which don't work for me) or project lists (which I know I'll lose), I put each ongoing project onto a separate tray of my baker's rack. Now if I want to create a newsletter or do research for a book or write an article or press release, I simply pull the corresponding tray from the rack and carry it to my desk.

Bathrooms

Problem: My son keeps missing the toilet.

Try this: Drain the bowl, dry a spot on the enamel down low near the center of the toilet, and paint on a circle of brightly colored fingernail polish. Once it dries, refill the bowl. Tell him that's his target from now on. The polish will eventually wear off, but by then he won't need it.

Hallway

Problem: My linen closet is always a mess.

Try this: Maybe you have too many linens. Two to three sets of sheets per bed is plenty; anything more than that makes clutter.

The best organizational system I have found is to slide a complete set of sheets into one of its matching pillowcases. That way whenever you need a new set of sheets, you simply grab and go.

One more tip for a neater linen closet, and this is one of those housekeeping impaired no-brainers that it only took me 40-some years to figure out: *Folding looks much neater when it's done against a flat surface rather than in the air.* I never could figure out why my housekeeper's folding was so much better than mine until I realized she was smoothing each item out on a tabletop as she folded. I, on the other hand, was standing in the middle of the room, folding my towels in front of me without benefit of a surface. There is a marked difference in results.

Bedrooms

Problem: The trash in my son's room never quite makes it to the trash can.

Try this: Install a toy basketball hoop on the wall, about a foot above the can. See if that doesn't motivate him to try, try again.

Problem: My kids don't do a good job making their beds, and their covers always end up looking lumpy.

Try this: Hey, at least they're doing something! If the beds look messy even when made, consider getting a different comforter or bedspread. In my experience, the thicker the comforter, the more forgiving it is of the bumpy blankets and sheets underneath. Just make sure you never buy any bedding that's bigger than your washing machine can hold.

Problem: My teenage daughter's dresser top is constantly cluttered with beauty products.

Try this: Of course it is. She's a teenager. The most you can do is make a few helpful suggestions, but leave it to her whether she wants to implement changes or not. Remember that she probably doesn't want it to be messy either and would welcome the chance to come up with her own strategies.

Suggest she move the dresser to the opposite wall, out of the Sight Zone. Some attractive containers and plastic baskets may help her get organized as well.

Problem: I never seem to put away my jewelry.

Try this: If your jewelry box isn't working for you, it may be because you are a nonhook person trying to utilize a hook-required system.

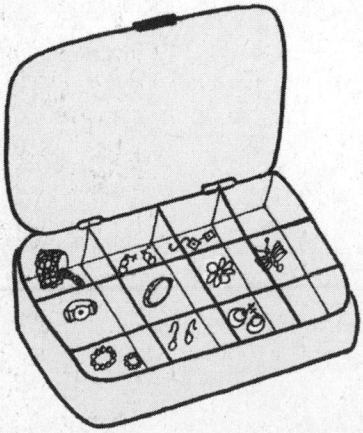

Ditch anything that forces you to hang up your earrings or necklaces in order to put them away. Get some clear holders with individual compartments instead. I found my jewelry holders in the "Organizing Section" of an office supply store. Now my jewelry stays neat and clean because I can see what I want without having to touch everything as I sort through them.

Garage/Shed

Problem: My kids leave their bicycles and scooters in the wrong places.

Try this: Paint individual parking spots for them on the garage floor.

Car

Problem: The inside of my car is always a mess.

Try this: Treat the interior of your car like a room in a house. That means give it a small trash can (forget those wimpy plastic bags that hang from the doors, you need an open one that'a more convenient to use), set up Stations, and use attractive containers and an occasional purging to keep a handle on clutter and mess. Keep a pack of glass wipes in your glove compartment, and make vacuuming a regular part of your car-care routine.

Problem: The outside of my car always looks dirty.

Try this: The next time you buy a car, bear this in mind. The best colors for hiding dirt and dust are light, such as silver, light gold, and even white. The colors that show dirt the most are dark, such as black and dark blue.

Backyard/Deck/Patio

Problem: The front porch needs sweeping regularly, but I don't want to get my good broom dirty.

Try this: Every home should have two brooms: an exterior one and an interior one. Make sure they look completely different so no one confuses the two.

Problem: Kids play in the dirt and mud and then track it into the house.

Try this: Install an outdoor hose shower near the back door for quick rinse downs of dirty kids...or at least their shoes. Another idea is to have their "outside" shoes stay outside in a storage chest or in the garage.

Problem: Kids get mud and grass into the pool when they climb in and out.

Try this: Keep a plastic dishpan next to the pool. Whenever the kids go swimming have them fill it with a big scoop of pool water. Set it next to the ladder or steps. Before they climb in, they can rinse their feet in the dishpan.

Really Thinking Outside the Box

For some creative people, the sky's the limit when it comes to inventing ways to adapt their house to the HTCI System. Enjoy these "what if" suggestions for conquering messes.

If I Built a House That Cleans Itself from Scratch...

- "I would install a conveyor belt in the garage that runs right through an automatic doorway to the kitchen. That way when I come home from the grocery store, I could just take my items out of the trunk and set them on the belt, turn it on, and meet my groceries inside."
- "I would take a cue from the old days and put in a dumbwaiter to make it easier to move items from the first floor to the second and vice versa. I don't know why they ever stopped making dumbwaiters. I think they're really smart."
- "I would include a tile bay with a hose and drain right in the kitchen. At mealtimes I would put my son's high chair in the bay and let him eat there. When he was finished, I would hose down him and the chair—and let the mess simply wash down the drain!"
- "I would put the laundry room upstairs, located in the middle of all the bedrooms like a hub of a wheel. When

clothes are ready to put away, I would simply slide open doors to reveal the insides of the various bedroom closets. No more carrying baskets of laundry up and down stairs for me!"

- "I would want some sort of barcode scanning system for the fridge and pantry so I could always know the inventory of the food I have on hand by scanning items as I put them in or take them out."
- "I would build 'false walls' at the backs of my kitchen counters, ones that could slide open to reveal the small appliances neatly tucked away behind them. I would have electrical outlets in there too so the appliances would always be ready to use."

Handy Lists for Quick Reference

10 Principles of a House That Cleans Itself

1. Change the house to fit the behavior.
2. Change the behavior to fit the house, but only after you've changed the house as much as possible.
3. Control your "expected messy areas" and "Sight Zones."
4. Think "Up and Away."
5. Think like a housecleaning service.
6. Emphasize simplicity.
7. Engineer convenience.
8. Utilize the power of beauty.
9. Camouflage wherever possible.
10. Do everything with an eye toward maintenance.

The CONVERT System

C lear out the clutter

O pen up and clean

N eaten, organize, and solve problem spots

V erify Rabbit Trails and set up Stations

E xamine Sight Zones

R ecord future improvements needed

T ake steps now for ongoing maintenance

The Three Rules for Creating Stations

1. All related items need to be identified and collected.
2. This collection needs to be placed in a single container, in an appropriate storage area, in the room where you're most likely to perform the task.
3. The tools in a Station should never be removed from that Station.

The Four Elements of Ongoing Maintenance

1. Anticipate "illegal parkers."
2. Anticipate trash.
3. Anticipate purging.
4. Anticipate dirt.

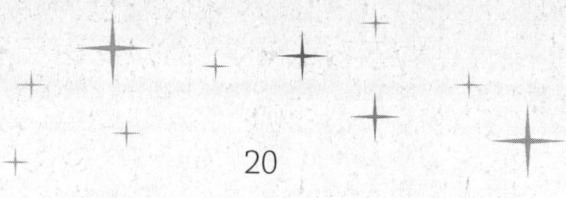

20

How to Clean a House That Cleans Itself

Perseverance must finish its work so that you may be mature and complete, not lacking anything.

JAMES 1:4

Okay, you've established the three cleaning Stations: Quick Clean, Intermediate Clean, and Deep Clean. It's time to put them to use and keep your clean home sparkling for good.

Learning to Quick Clean

How long do you think it takes to unload the dishwasher? Fold a load of laundry? Clean a toilet? If you are housekeeping impaired, chances are you grossly overestimate the time needed for many household tasks. Working at a normal speed, these three jobs take about three minutes each.

How about wiping fingerprints from the front of the refrigerator? Changing out dirty towels for clean ones in the bathroom? Dusting a ceiling fan?

If your home is set up with easily accessible cleaning tools, each of these jobs require less than a minute and sometimes as little as 30 seconds. If you think about the number of times in any given day you have anywhere from 30 seconds to 4 minutes to spare, you'll grasp the importance of this concept: Quick cleaning is the single best way to stay on top of household messes.

Let's take a look at time. Think of the things you do in a day that require waiting:

- cooking a frozen dinner in the microwave
- being on hold on the telephone
- waiting for the school bus to come
- listening to a song on the radio
- waiting at the door for the dog to come inside
- waiting for your kids to finish brushing their teeth so you can tuck them in
- waiting for the water in the shower to heat up

In terms of tiny segments of time, it's quite possible to teach yourself to match brief opportunities of "waiting time" with "just as briefly accomplished" cleaning tasks. For example, it takes me about three minutes to unload my dishwasher. It also takes three minutes to cook my favorite frozen meal for lunch. Whenever I start the microwave for three minutes, I make myself load or unload the dishwasher as my meal is cooking.

In a House That Cleans Itself, random moments of brief cleaning are a vital part of what keeps the house clean.

To the average person this is a no-brainer. But to the housekeeping impaired, it feels strange indeed. In the past I would have spent those three minutes frittering around the kitchen, maybe flipping through a pile of mail, glancing at a mail-order catalog, checking my voice mail, or even just standing there channel-flipping on the kitchen television. Why wouldn't I have spent that time cleaning? As the housekeeping impaired person might say,

- "I'm already busy cooking, and I can't clean if I'm already doing something else."
- "This isn't my cleaning time. I only clean when I have the time to do it right and do it completely."
- "It never crossed my mind" or "I didn't even notice that it needed doing."

There are plenty of reasons that some folks don't naturally seize random little moments available to them throughout the day and use those for cleaning. But *in a House That Cleans Itself, random moments of brief cleaning are a vital part of what keeps the house clean.* We just have to teach ourselves to take advantage of the time that comes our way.

To that end, your next job is to grab your notebook, a pen or pencil, and a stopwatch. (If you don't have a stopwatch, use a digital timer or a watch with a second hand.) You can do this by yourself, but it's also a fun activity with children. For younger children, they can yell "Go!" and press the start button; for older children, you can take turns timing each other.

Whether working alone or accompanied, go to area #1 on your Flow Plan—the entryway. In your notebook write down a list of tasks that would qualify as quick cleaning for this area. These may include:

- wipe down door and door frame
- shake dirt out of floor mat
- clean glass with glass-cleaning wipes
- dust furniture with dusting wipes
- water plant
- dust light fixture
- sweep and mop up tracked-in dirt

Once you have made a full list, time yourself or have someone time you as you do the first task on the list. Here's what you do:

1. Stand in the middle of the room

2. Start timer
3. Retrieve the product(s) needed to do the first task on the list. Most products should be in your Quick Clean or Intermediate Clean Stations, though this can also include getting a cup of water from the kitchen to water a plant or getting a pair of shoes to go outside to shake out a dirty floor mat.
4. Do the first task on the list, moving no more quickly or slowly than you would on any given day as you would normally perform this task
5. When the task is complete, put away cleaning tools
6. Throw away any trash generated, such as dirty wipes
7. Return to the middle of the room
8. Stop the timer

Now write down how long that task took. Repeat the eight steps for every task on the list. When you are finished, your list may look like this:

- wipe down door and door frame—30 seconds
- shake dirt out of floor mat—1 minute, 6 seconds
- clean glass with glass-cleaning wipes—42 seconds
- dust furniture with dusting wipes—1 minute, 12 seconds
- water plant—45 seconds
- dust light fixture—18 seconds
- sweep and mop up tracked-in dirt—2 minutes, 15 seconds

You may be surprised at how quickly most of these tasks can be accomplished, which is good because that's the point. By taking a vague all-or-nothing concept like "clean the house" and turning it into much smaller, more specific tasks with times assigned, such as an 18-second action of retrieving the long-handled duster, running it over the light fixture, and returning the duster to the closet, you make quick cleaning a painless, nonintimidating prospect that can be done in stolen moments during the day.

But there's one more step to this exercise—one that will go a long way toward your succeeding in your new quick clean mentality. After you have gone into each area, listed the quick clean tasks for that area and timed them, take the data you have compiled and put it into individual lists suitable for posting. Rearrange the list of tasks for each area in order of length, from quickest to longest. For example, our sample list would now read:

Entryway

Dust light fixture . . . . . 18 seconds

Wipe down door and door frame . . . . . 30 seconds

Clean glass with glass-cleaning wipes . . 42 seconds

Water plant . . . . . 45 seconds

Shake dirt out of floor mat. . . . . 1 minute, 6 seconds

Dust furniture with dusting wipes. . . . . 1 minute, 12 seconds

Sweep and mop up tracked-in dirt . . . . . 2 minutes, 15 seconds

After you have made a separate list like this for every area in your house, find a place in each area to post it that is out of sight but convenient to get to. Hang your lists inside closet or cabinet doors or tuck into the Quick Clean Stations alongside your cleaning supplies. (You may want to laminate the lists first.) In every area you now have a complete list of the little random jobs that can be done whenever necessary, along with the amount of time required to do those jobs.

The next step is to link these tasks with spare moments throughout the day so you will remember to do them. Train yourself to use "markers" to jog your memory. For example, if you regularly wait for something in that area, pass through it at certain times of the day, or even make it part of a first-thing-in-the-morning or last-thing-in-the-evening routine, associate what you're doing with a task. Before you know it, the act of brushing your teeth will remind you to wipe down the bathroom counter, getting up in the morning will include making your bed, and waiting to tuck in your kids at night can mean a quick straightening of the sheets and towels in the linen closet.

At the very least, whenever you find yourself with a few minutes to spare, check a list of quick clean tasks and pick one or two that will fit your time. That way even if you only have "two minutes to spare," as we so often do, you can use those minutes efficiently and easily by letting the list be your guide.

Remember too that this list isn't just for you. It's for *every* person who lives in your house who is old enough and capable enough to clean. Train everyone to utilize the list throughout the day. You'll soon be amazed at how many messes disappear. For younger children, get them started in this practice by making a second list tailored just for them. Snap some photos of them doing specific tasks, such as putting away their bathtub toys or wiping the lower cabinets with a wet washcloth. Put the photos on the fridge and praise your kids for their work. Train those kids up in the way they should go, and when they are grown, they won't be housekeeping impaired!

For older children and teens who aren't accustomed to thinking about cleaning at all, I suggest you give them tasks in a given area that relates to a specific part of their day. For example, if your daughter likes to talk on the phone, make her the official telephone cleaner. Stash a packet of wipes within easy reach and remind her to use them when she's talking. She can wipe down the telephone and the surrounding area. If your son enjoys playing basketball in the driveway, make it his job to sweep the front walk when he goes out to play.

Before and After

As you have probably realized by now, quick cleaning has less to do with a physical act and more to do with a mental one. Because you have already gone to the trouble to CONVERT your home to a

House That Cleans Itself, these changes are now far easier to make and to integrate into your routine.

Still need convincing? Consider this example for the task of cleaning a dirty mat and floor near the door *before CONVERTing to a House That Cleans Itself.*

Task	Time
✦ put on shoes (Where are my shoes? Has anyone seen my shoes? Find shoes. Need to sit down to put on shoes but nowhere to sit because of the clutter. Move clutter to table, sit on chair, put on shoes, return to entryway with shoes on)	2 minutes
✦ pick up floor mat, carry it out the front door, shake dirt onto the grass. (Unfortunately, this hasn't been done in so long that the shaking takes a while.)	45 seconds
✦ bring floor mat back inside and put it down nearby but out of the way	10 seconds
✦ gather broom, dustpan, mop, bucket, cleaner, and water (cleaning closet is a mess, can't find the right cleaner, dustpan is missing, finally find everything, have to fill bucket at the sink and add cleaner, kitchen sink is full of dirty dishes so have to do it in bathroom, return to entryway with all tools)	4 minutes
✦ sweep the floor, scoop dirt into dustpan, dump dirt (trash can is four rooms away, have to walk in there to dump dustpan)	1 minute, 55 seconds
✦ put away broom and dustpan (shove them back into the closet)	5 seconds
✦ mop the floor	1 min., 15 sec.
✦ pour out mop water (would be faster to pour it into the sink, but the sink is full of dirty dishes	39 seconds

so carry bucket to the bathroom and dump into toilet)	
✦ put tools away	5 seconds
✦ when floor is dry, place mat in front of door	3 seconds
Total time required to complete tasks:	10 minutes, 55 seconds

After CONVERTing to a House That Cleans Itself:

Task	Time
✦ put on shoes, which are stored in the entryway, near a bench where you can sit to slip them on	25 seconds
✦ pick up floor mat, carry it out the front door, shake the dirt onto grass	28 seconds
✦ bring floor mat back inside and put it down nearby but out of the way	10 seconds
✦ gather rechargeable vacuum and instant mop from Intermediate Clean Station	10 seconds
✦ vacuum floor, dump tray in trash can, which is in next room	1 minute, 5 seconds
✦ mop the floor with instant mop	50 seconds
✦ put tools neatly away	10 seconds
✦ when floor is dry, place mat in front of door	3 seconds
Total time required to complete tasks:	3 minutes, 21 seconds

What is the difference between more than 10 minutes and less than 4 minutes? If you are housekeeping impaired, that's the difference between a difficult chore that rarely gets done and a simple habit that is easily integrated into your life. Stop waiting for that "perfect" moment to do a massive, wonderful cleaning. Those perfect moments rarely come as often as they should, and in the meantime your house is growing less and less perfect by the day.

Learning to Deep Clean

No matter how much we don't want to think about it, now and then every house needs more than just a quick clean—even a house that cleans itself. Deep cleaning may never be your forte, but at least the difference between deep cleaning now and the way deep cleaning went before your conversion will probably be extraordinary. Why? Because in the past much of your "cleaning" time wasn't spent cleaning at all. It was spent neatening, shuffling clutter, and gathering your cleaning supplies. Imagine setting out to deep clean with easy-to-find tools in an already neat house. Is that a radical thought? For the housekeeping impaired, it might have been before, but not any longer! Get ready to live the way those "other" people live, where deep cleaning is a normal weekly task that requires no more or less effort than it ought to.

There are many different approaches to take with the who's, how's, and when's of deep cleaning. After much research and trial and error, I have settled upon three favorite methods for the housekeeping impaired to handle the deep cleaning. I suggest you try all three to find out which one is the most successful for you and your family members.

1. *Room Ownership*—best for a home whose room count is no more than twice the number of people who live there (i.e., a single person with a 2-room apartment, a family of three with a 6-room house)
2. *Day Division*—best for singles and smaller families
3. *Room to Room Sequencing*—good for a home with at least four capable family members (such as two adults and two teens) and can include younger family members as well

Room Ownership

When my kids were younger, the hardest part of getting them to help around the house was the "blame game." For every five things I told them to pick up or put away, three of those had nothing to do with them, so theybalked when told to clean. "But *she* left it there. Tell *her* to clean it!" "That mess is *hers,* not mine!" On and on it went.

Yes, we had a few lessons about the basic family dynamic of all for one and one for all, but still I had to admit there was a certain logic to their complaints. If they were both in a room when it got messy but one simply dropped a few books on the floor and the other left out a bunch of dirty plates and spilled cracker crumbs from one end of the couch to the other, where was the fairness in giving them an equal load in cleaning?

On the other hand, why should I have to be the one to divide out and enforce individual responsibility? I just wanted the room clean regardless of who messed it up. The blame game used to make me nuts.

Then I discovered the Room Ownership principle. In Room Ownership, the various common rooms of the house are assigned to different family members. It is their job to see that the room stays neat during the week and gets its deep cleaning at the end of the week. That's a fairly common division of responsibility for big families, but here is our twist: The person who "owned" that room was not necessarily required to clean everything in that room but merely held the chief responsibility of seeing that it got cleaned. Therefore, if big sister owns the family room but in that family room is a big mess made by little sister, it's big sister's job to go and get little sister and have her clean up the mess she made.

It sounds simple, but this method does more than just get rooms clean. It takes the parents out of the roll of arbiter and enforcer; it slowly teaches kids to be more considerate of other people's spaces; it allows people to become familiar with the responsibilities of getting specific and limited areas clean, thus making them more efficient;

and finally it tends to give the owners a certain sense of pride in the rooms, which makes them more likely to keep them clean.

There are a few basic rules for Room Ownership.

1. If someone has made a mess in your room, you may go get him and have him clean up that mess, but you must not do it in a disrespectful manner. You may also choose to give him a break and simply clean his mess yourself. It's your choice, but it must be done without resentment or sharp words.
2. If someone comes and gets you and says you left a mess in her room, you must stop what you're doing if at all possible and go and fix the mess you made in her room.
3. Rooms should be assigned based on age and ability. Generally, mom will take the kitchen and dining room, dad will handle the exterior yard and structures and cars, and the kids will divide out the family room, bathrooms, entryway, and hallways.
4. If there are younger children in the house, they can be assigned as a "room buddy" and given simple tasks. Even a toddler knows when he is part of the family cleaning routine. He can help by dusting the baseboards and lower cabinets with a dry rag. (He might miss a few spots, but he's sure building a great habit.)
5. Each person is responsible for organizing and replenishing the cleaning tools needed for their room. (Requests for cleaning products can be written on the master shopping list on the fridge.) To help build enthusiasm, each person should be allowed to buy a cleaning-tool carrier of his choice for storing his tools. He may want a bright-red plastic bin, a handled caddy, or even a carpenter's apron. (A kid in a carpenter's apron that has been fully stocked with spray cleaners, paper towels, and rags is a force to be reckoned with and a great soldier in the battle against grime.)

6. To prevent conflicts over sharing vacuum cleaners, mops, etc., general times or days should be assigned in a staggered fashion.

What deep cleaning tasks should be done in each room? In general, once a week or at least once every other week the rooms should be cleaned as follows.

Family Room

- clean in or around fireplace as needed
- dust all furniture
- clean all glass and metal
- vacuum floors and all upholstered furniture
- vacuum or run duster high along the walls and around the rim of the ceiling
- mop any hardwood floors
- neatly arrange couch pillows, cushions, knickknacks, etc.
- empty trash

Kitchen

- disinfect countertops, backsplash, table, stove
- wipe all large appliances and small appliances; don't miss the inside of the microwave
- wipe all cabinet fronts and knobs
- wipe around doorways, light switches, air vents
- vacuum floor
- mop floor
- dry out sink
- toss old food from fridge
- wipe down inside of fridge
- wipe stove vent

Bedrooms

- strip linens and take to laundry room
- put on clean linens and make bed
- take dirty clothes to laundry room
- dust all furniture
- clean all visible glass, such as mirrors and prominent windows
- vacuum carpets
- mop hardwood floors
- vacuum underneath the bed and in the floors of closets
- dust tops of wood moldings around windows and doors

Bathrooms

- spray and wipe toilet and toilet bowl
- spray and wipe sink and base
- spray and wipe tub and shower
- clean all glass and metal
- wipe walls around sink area, toilet area, and bath area
- vacuum floor
- mop the floor with disinfectant
- hang fresh towels and take dirty ones to laundry room
- replenish toilet paper as needed
- straighten magazines, shelves, etc., as needed

Other areas

- neatening
- dusting
- glass, metal, and electronics cleaning
- vacuuming
- mopping

About once a month, you should:

- wipe the top of the fridge
- clean the less visible windows
- dust all lampshades and ceiling fans

About once every three months, you should also:

- wash comforters, bedspreads, and pillows
- clear out and clean under the bathroom sink
- clean out the medicine cabinet
- dust all miniblinds
- clean most-visible windows inside and out

About every six months, you should

- wash curtains
- air out house
- have rugs cleaned
- hose down the front porch, house exterior, and garage door
- clean less-visible windows inside and out

If you choose the Room Ownership method for deep cleaning, make sure you make a list of the tasks required for each room. Family members will be handling those lists as they clean, so you might want to laminate them. Go over the list with each owner, one on one, to make sure the person understands how to do all jobs. For consistency, advise your cleaners always to work from left to right and top to bottom, just like the housecleaning experts do.

With the Room Ownership method, it's important to find a fun but fair way to choose who gets what room. Different family members will often gravitate toward different room choices on their own. But if the division doesn't happen naturally, make it a game to decide who will be doing what. Buy as many candy bars (or something more healthful if you prefer) as there are rooms and write on the back of each bar the name of a room. Spread out the bars on a table and let everyone pick two. They get to keep the candy and those rooms. Swaps are allowed when mutually agreeable.

Finally, put a time limit on Room Ownership, usually one month, so that no one is stuck with the more difficult rooms for long. This way every family member eventually has a chance to learn how to clean each room in the house.

Day Division Method

Day Division is a good choice for cleaning when the bulk of the work falls to one or two people, especially if those people are quite busy with other parts of their lives. With Day Division, there is no single day of deep cleaning. Instead, the cleaning is divided into six separate chunks, each of which is accomplished on a different day of the week.

There is nothing new about this system. Having a specific "laundry day," for example, probably started when Adam and Eve traded in their fig leaves for animal skins. ("Adam, it's Monday so I'll be down at the river beating that rabbit fur with a stick. Cain, stop picking on your brother!") Nowadays Day Division Cleaning may appeal to you if you work at a job all week and don't want to sacrifice the bulk of your day off to getting your house under control.

To set up your own Day Division System, write down in broad terms the tasks required to deep-clean your house, such as vacuum, mop, dust, glass cleaning, horizontal wiping with cloth and cleaner, vertical wiping with cloth and cleaner, laundry, clean out fridge, toilets, tubs and showers, sweeping exteriors, windows, empty trash.

In your notebook draw six columns and label them with the days of the week, Monday through Saturday. Looking at your list of tasks, assign the more obvious ones where they would fall. For example, if you like to cook on Fridays, put cooking there—and make a week's worth of meals on that single day. If you like to start the week with clean laundry, make Saturday your laundry day. When you are finished giving each day a task, your chart might look like this:

Monday	Tuesday	Wednesday	Thursday	Friday	Saturday
tubs & toilets	dust & glass	vert. wiping	mop	cooking	laundry
trash	horiz. wiping	vacuum	trash	clean fridge	exteriors
			grocery shop	clean stove	cars

Make sure that certain tasks precede others. For example, you want to wipe and dust prior to vacuuming, and you want to vacuum prior to mopping.

This system may or may not appeal to you. For some, it's such a relief to avoid a single big three-or-four-hour cleaning day that cleaning a little bit each day is a great relief. For others, spreading the job out like this makes them feel like they are always cleaning, so it doesn't work as well. (For me, the biggest drawback of this method is that when my family does it this way, we don't get that "deep clean euphoria" payoff that comes when strolling through a spotless house after several concentrated hours of hard work.)

If you decide to try the Day Division method of cleaning, feel free to tweak your list on a weekly basis until you feel it is working best for you. (For example, if you usually work late on Wednesdays, move one of those tasks to Tuesdays and the other to Thursdays.) You might also consider using this system every *other* week rather than weekly if your home doesn't get that dirty in-between.

Day Division cleaning is worth trying for a month or so. If you find that having a short, near-daily deep cleaning session feels like less work than a longer, single, weekly deep cleaning session would, this is probably the best plan for you.

Room-to-Room Sequence Cleaning

In my household, Room-to-Room Sequencing is our cleaning method of choice. It works for us because, at 15 and 17, our children are old enough to handle any cleaning task that our house requires. It's especially good when we are tempted to drag on too long with cleaning or get sidetracked while cleaning because the way this system works, neither of those things can happen. Some other big plusses for this system are:

- the work moves very quickly because there's a certain urgency that comes from being followed
- no one feels like he or she is getting a bum rap because everyone works equally hard
- it truly makes you feel like a team eagerly striving toward a common goal

A big minus of this system is that it can take longer to get set up and rolling in the beginning. I was shocked to find that it took me an entire day to go from room to room in my house writing down all necessary cleaning tasks in specific detail, and then charting out what each person's responsibilities were for each room. It was like working out the pieces of a big puzzle. When it finally came together, it did so beautifully. Here's how it's done.

Each person is assigned a number and several primary tasks:

1. Dad—neatener, preparer, high duster
2. Mom—wiper, disinfectant sprayer, tub scrubber
3. Teen A—vacuumer, toilet cleaner
4. Teen B—mopper, finisher

Next, each person is given a list of rooms in a specific order and the tasks they are to complete in each room. At the words "Let's go," each person takes his list in hand and begins to work through it. The lists are carefully coordinated so there are no traffic jams, and everyone is making a full sweep around the house in a very specific sequence.

For example, while person #1 is gathering supplies from the

cleaning closet, person #2 is stripping the sheets from all of the beds, person #3 is doing the dishes, and person #4 is gathering up the dirty laundry in the house and carrying it to the laundry room. When person #1 has his supplies, he moves into the first room and begins his share of the cleaning:

- Straightening up any mess, putting anything that belongs elsewhere in a laundry basket for redistributing.
- Preparing the room for the vacuumer and mopper by clearing the way—removing knickknacks and other items from tables and desks and picking up smaller things from the floor such as baskets or floor mats (each room should have a prearranged place for those items to be clustered temporarily, such as on the couch or a chair).
- Running an extended-reach ostrich feather duster along the tops of cabinets, high shelves, upper walls, and ceiling.

When he is finished with those three tasks, he calls out "Done!" and moves into the next room, where he does the same basic actions again. He will proceed throughout the house, attacking each new space in order as the neatener, preparer, and high duster.

Meanwhile, as soon as #1 finishes in a room and shouts that he is done, person #2 moves right into that room and starts her work. As the designated wiper, disinfectant sprayer, and tub scrubber, she will be dusting and wiping all surfaces, cleaning all glass, and scrubbing all showers and tubs as she comes to them.

As soon as she is finished with a room, she moves on to the next one, and person #3 takes her place. As the vacuumer and toilet cleaner, her job is fairly straightforward.

Finally, when person #3 is ready to move on, person #4 goes to that room and starts her work. Number 4's tasks include "finishing"—putting back all the things that person #1 moved off of tables and counters such as knickknacks and baskets, replacing hand towels where needed, replenishing toilet paper and tissues, etc. Once the space looks lovely and is completely put back together, she dumps the trash into a big bag that she carries with her, mops the floor, and turns off the light.

As you can see by now, what's happening throughout the house is that each room is getting cleaned by four different people, one at a time, in a row, with each person doing different tasks. By the time person #4 moves into the second room to repeat her tasks there, person #3 is working in the third room, person #2 is in the fourth room, and person #1 is in the fifth room. This sort of room-by-room sequencing continues throughout the house until the entire place sparkles from top to bottom.

This system seems the most complicated on paper, but once it is put into action it becomes much simpler. The hardest part is timing tasks to prevent traffic jams. That is best done by observing where those jams tend to happen (like person #1 is still doing his job in the kitchen when person #2 moves in and starts her job, and she is quickly followed by person #3, who is ready to do her job but can't because 1 and 2 are in her way). This happens because not every task takes as long in every room. Where the wiper might spend half an hour wiping down the cabinets, appliances, and counters in the kitchen, the vacuumer may only need 10 minutes in there. In the living room, on the other hand, the vacuumer may spend 20 minutes vacuuming pet hair from a difficult rug while the wiper just has to dust a few tables and breeze on through.

To prevent traffic jams, once you see when and where they happen, tweak each person's task list to slow them down or speed them up accordingly. For example, at the point where the mopper usually catches up with the vacuumer, her task list might say, "Check out back to see that the patio furniture is neat, the yard looks good, and sweep the deck." By the time she has done those tasks and comes back inside, there is no longer a backlog because the person ahead of her has finished and moved on.

If Room-to-Room Sequence Cleaning appeals to you, give it a try! Like a giant wave, it will wash through your entire house, leaving cleanliness in its wake. To motivate our teenagers, we agreed to take the money we would be saving on a housekeeper and apply it toward a big family trip. In our area, the going rate for housecleaners is around $100 per visit, so as you can imagine the savings piled up fairly quickly. A year later we were headed to Hawaii, where we gladly didn't have to clean a thing except the sand from the soles of our feet.

My Most Embarrassing Messy House Story

—A Hidden Unmentionable—

BY BETH

Several weeks after my teenage daughter had a sleepover, we found her friend's bra under the sofa. I don't know who was more embarrassed, the girl for losing it or me for not vacuuming under the sofa for so long.

21

Doing the Paper Two-Step

Good will come to him who is generous and lends freely, who conducts his affairs with justice.

PSALM 112:5

Want to get a handle on the paper clutter in your house? Try doing the Two-Step, which has been specifically designed for the housekeeping impaired. The Two-Step consists of, well, two steps: the quick sort, to be done daily, and the slow sort, to be done weekly. If you use a combination of these two systems, the paper problems in your home will be eliminated.

The Quick Sort

Establish a *Standing Paper Station* and *tell yourself that from now on, you're not allowed to look at a piece of paper unless you are standing beside the Station.* No more flipping through the mail as you come up the walk and then dumping it in a heap on the front hall table. Instead, collect the mail, walk to your Paper Station, and *then* look at it. You are far more likely to ditch the junk immediately if you are standing directly beside a trash can, recycle bin, and shredder the first time you see it.

Standing Paper Station

Some people associate the processing of paperwork with sitting at a desk when things are quiet and we can give those papers our undivided attention. What we fail to acknowledge is that most of the papers that come at us on a daily basis do so as the dog is barking, the kids are fighting, and dinner is boiling over. We shove those papers to the side, thinking we'll get to them later when we have peace and quiet and can sit at a desk. Give up that notion! Life can get crazy-busy, and rarely do the housekeeping impaired ever manage to develop the habit of making it to the desk. Instead, we need to set up a little triage station for our papers so we can do the primary sort in the midst of the chaos.

To create a Standing Paper Station, you'll need a trash can, a shredder, and eight containers or cubbyholes into which you will divide your papers. The key is that the action of sorting the papers is done from up to down—you drop the papers into each hole vertically, much like tossing them into the trash, rather than sliding them onto a horizontal shelf. That's why you'll probably want to eschew the standard "literature sorters" sold at office supply stores in favor of an eight-cubby shoe holder or wine rack turned sideways. These sorting bins need to be at a comfortable height for you to use while standing up. Ideally they should be placed along with your shredder and trash can on a three-shelf rolling cart.

If you use a rolling cart, keep it in a central location near a plug for the shredder so that it can be unplugged and rolled away when company's coming. Make sure there's a place nearby where it can be stashed, such as inside a closet. (Remember, to make life easier and ultimately neater, you're using two standards of clean—one for insiders, one for outsiders.) No matter how utilitarian, also keep in mind the maxim about beauty being a great motivator. If this contraption is ugly, you're going to avoid it. So make sure the Station is as nifty-looking as it is useful.

Label each of the eight cubbies as follows: *Money, Time, Possessions, Life, School, Work, Tools,* and *By Sunrise.* Into the *Tools* cubby, place the items you need for responding to urgent matters, including a checkbook, envelopes, stamps, return address stickers, a stapler, self-stick notes, a highlighter, tape, and a pen. Don't allow anyone to run off with these items. If they do, start tying the items down with strings.

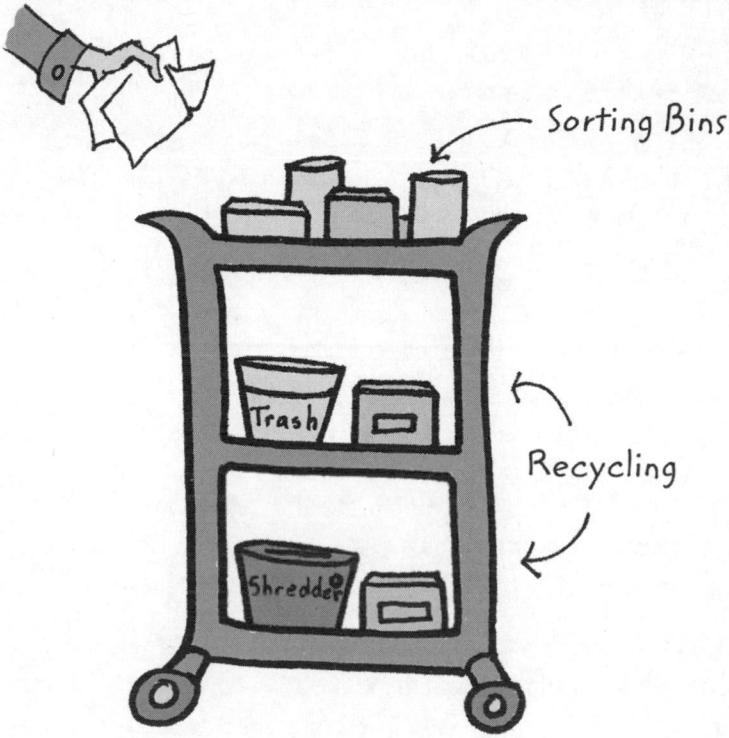

Whenever a piece of paper comes into your hand, walk to the Station and distribute it as follows:

- *Shredder*—if it's junk but has your name on it, put it through the shredder
- *Recycle*—if it's nonpersonalized junk and recyclable, put it in the recycle bin. (Check with your local recycle organizations to find out the guidelines for recycling in your area.)
- *Trash*—if it's junk but nonpersonalized and nonrecyclable, put it in the trash

- *Money*—for all papers related to bills, bank statements, pay stubs
- *Time*—for event notices, invitations, tickets, community class catalogs, ads from theaters, library schedules
- *Possessions*—for sale flyers, receipts, coupons, warranties, mail-order catalogs
- *Life*—for Cub Scout forms, address changes, decorating ideas, recipes, fitness, menus, political flyers, travel, mementos, maps, magazines
- *School*—for info on fund-raisers, teacher notes, report cards
- *Work*—invoices, business cards, resumes
- *By Sunrise*—permission slips that must be signed and returned, payments that must be urgently made, messages that must be returned. Be honest: If the cubby was called "Urgent," you might avoid it. By labeling it "By Sunrise," you know you must give it your attention either before you go to bed or the moment you get up.

If you are using a solid-unit cubby divider (such as a shoe or wine rack), then place a slightly smaller removable container inside the *By Sunrise* cubby. If you find that these items are not getting the attention they deserve, make a habit of moving that container to the center of the kitchen table each day when you start cooking supper. Attend to it in those spare moments when you're waiting for the water to boil or the oven to preheat. If necessary, tell yourself you must act on all items in the container before you are allowed to eat the dinner you're cooking.

One final note: If you become involved in an extensive-but-temporary major project such as buying a house, renovating, planning a wedding, or organizing an event, the related papers will accumulate at an astonishing rate. (By the time we finished renovating our kitchen, our stack of papers was more than 8" high!) Whenever you become involved in something like this, add a temporary basket or box to a lower shelf of your cart and use it for all papers related to the project. Otherwise they will clog the other cubbies and have to be resorted back out again later.

Doing the Slow Sort

The next step in the Two-Step Sort System can be fairly painful. Once a week you must clear out *all* cubbies (except the *Tools* one) and further sort all items. If you have a file-friendly spouse or teen, by all means delegate this task to him or her!

If family members are as hopeless with files as you are, try doing this together or, at the very least, under the "supervision" of a friend or a school-aged child. Even if said child is simply sitting at a nearby table doing homework, his or her presence can be a constant reminder that you need to focus and complete this task. Give the family member the assignment of keeping you on track. Even the youngest assistant will gleefully guard your wandering eyes and too-long pauses with gentle reminders, such as, "Dad! Stop reading that mail-order catalog and get back to work!"

To further sort each category, use a combination of bins, containers, and, yes, hanging file folders. You know the types of papers that come through your house, so this is a system you will have to play with over the course of several months to get it fine-tuned. In general, think always in terms of making things easier on yourself. The less you have to pause and think as you use this system in the future, the better.

Just as you created a Standing Paper Station, you now need to assemble a *Sitting Paper Station*. You probably already have a desk or side table that's supposed to be for handling household matters, but if you don't, it's time to get one. We tend to think in terms of desks as they relate to the business world, forgetting that the running of a household also requires an enormous amount of paperwork. For years I've had a full office upstairs for my writing business—and not so much as a card table downstairs for handling the business of life. No wonder my personal papers were a mess!

Your household desk area must be left alone by everyone except you and your spouse, which means one of two things: Either it's put in a very out-of-the-way location where no one else will even think of bothering it or it's set up in such a way that it has doors to close when it's not in use. If you don't want your desk tucked away in a spare bedroom, set it up in a main closet, if possible, making sure everything fits inside when the doors are closed. If you don't have a closet like that, consider buying a home-office armoire or closing office desk. Customize the interior spaces to fit your needs. When using your household desk, you need to function like a well-oiled machine.

After much deliberation (and some careful shopping because they weren't cheap), we bought a closing desk armoire. We chose a style and wood that matched our china cabinet and dining table. The armoire went against a free wall in the dining room. It looks beautiful when closed and functional when open. I absolutely love it.

Create a paper processing system that's just complicated enough to be effective and just simple enough to be doable.

I customized the interior by hanging a white board on the inside of the door along with three separate cork boards labeled "Commitments," "Possibilities," and "Miscellaneous." I also labeled the various shelves and cubbies, hung up the family calendar, and established a place inside that cabinet for everything that's going to be put there. Because file folders are like a black hole to me, the key to my success has been to use them only for "dead" items—those things I have to save in case I need them for tax and permanent record purposes, but otherwise I will never do anything with again. Any "live" item—one that still needs an action—goes into something other than a file.

As long as I am diligent about doing my once-a-week slow sort, the papers stay under control.

When you slow sort, you are going to move the papers that came in during the week into more specifically labeled areas. The goal is to *create a paper processing system that's just complicated enough to be effective and simple enough to be doable.* Remember, also, that you continue to shred, throw things in the trash, and recycle all along the way, so make sure to keep those bins handy at all times.

Divide the items in your *Money* cubby into *papers that need an action* (bills, bank statements), which you will move to the proper receptacle in your *Bill Paying Station,* and *those that don't* (pay stubs, investment records, Social Security info), which will go into file folders labeled for their different categories. You may want to look into using a rolling file cabinet to make life easier if you pay the bills in a different area than where you sort the mail.

Divide the items in your *Time* cubby into *Upcoming Commitments* (invitations, tickets, event notices) and *Upcoming Possibilities* (community class catalogs, ads from theaters, library schedules). Enter the info about the upcoming commitments on your calendar, and then put these items on a bulletin board where they can serve as reminders. Place the upcoming possibilities on a separate bulletin board (or different section of the same bulletin board) so that you can easily reach for them if you need them. Be sure to check both bulletin boards once a month and pull off any item whose date has passed. If there are any upcoming possibilities you sincerely hope not to miss, make a note of the dates on your calendar as well.

The items in your *Possessions* cubby require a double sort. First, separate the items into four separate piles: Sale flyers & Coupons, Mail-Order Catalogs, Receipts, and Other. Second, quickly go through each pile and throw out as much as you can, such as flyers for sales you're not going to get to, coupons for items you don't want, mail-order catalogs you won't read. After you have purged as much as possible, put the catalogs into your "catalog box." This should be a clear container with a lid that can hold a finite amount of catalogs.

Allow yourself to keep only as many catalogs as will fit in that box. If the box is full and some new ones come in that you want, you have to make room by tossing out some of the old. Personally, I love flipping through mail-order catalogs, but I have to stay on top of the quantity I keep around or they quickly multiply out of control. The clear box helps me do that.

Ditto with sale flyers and coupons. Place them in a clear, lidded "sale box," but do not allow the quantity to exceed the capacity of that box. If you have a better system for keeping coupons, by all means use it. But if you're like most housekeeping impaired people, coupons are more of a burden than a blessing because you don't know how to store them. And even when you do, you don't remember to take them to the store. (There's something about coupons that makes folks like us go into sorting hyper-drive, wasting time organizing by category, expiration date, etc.) If coupons give you grief, ditch the "coupon guilt" and eliminate them from your life entirely.

For receipts, take the highlighter and quickly mark the date, place, and form of payment on each one. Then separate them into three payment piles—credit cards, check/ATM, and cash. As you do, throw away any cash receipts for nondeductible expenses on nonreturnable items, like the salad you had at the food court while shopping in the mall. Pull out any major purchase receipts (in our house that's single items costing more than $100), and file them accordingly. Also pull out the receipts for any business or organization expenses that need reimbursement, write "Submit" across the top, and put them in your Bill Paying Station to take care of the next time you pay bills.

Paper-clip each of the three piles and drop them into the corresponding month of a 12-pocket, expanding file folder that is stored in your desk. Over the next few months, if you need to go back and verify an ATM withdrawal or a credit card charge, or if you need to return an item to a store, you should be able to find the receipt you need fairly easily by looking through that form of payment in that particular month. At the end of the year, when you pull together your records to do your taxes, most of these receipts can be thrown away. Just be sure to keep receipts for all home improvements, appliances, furniture, repairs, medical expenses, business expenses, and tax issues.

Deal with the items in the Other pile however you prefer. File, throw away, or whatever the situation calls for. Remember to put "dead" items you must keep in file folders and "live" items in other types of storage that you will more easily remember to check.

Divide the items in your *Life* cubby into related piles. For example, label clear plastic boxes as follows: "Things Requiring Action Now" (like forms that need to be filled out and sent in), "Things Requiring Action Later" (like change-of-address cards that need to be loaded into your computer or rolodex), "To Be Filed" (like decorating ideas, interesting articles, newspaper clippings), "Recipes," "Schedules," "To Read," "Maps," "Scrapbook," "Magazines," etc. Use each box for it's designated purpose, allowing the capacity of the box to determine how often you process and/or purge items. When a box is full, you *must* act on the items inside.

Put the maps into a map drawer and the magazines wherever you keep reading material. Schedules, such as the exercise class schedule for your gym or the practice schedule for your child's school play or sports team should go on your bulletin board. For recipes, try using a peel-and-stick photo album or a card-size file box, whichever works best for you.

Finally, for scrapbook items, you will probably need to carry them to a different location. Somewhere in your house, in a place that's easily accessible but not in the main traffic flow, each family member should have one big Rubbermaid-type container with a lid. Put into these containers their mementos, artwork, and other sentimental treasures. Once a year go through these bins as a family and weed out the items no longer important. Allow the size of the bin to determine the amount of items that may be saved over the span of the next 15 years. At some point put the stuff in scrapbooks if you enjoy doing that, but don't think scrapbooks are necessary. Years from now you will have just as much fun flipping through items in a box as you would turning through pages in a book.

Ditch This "Ought"

I ought to put my mementos into a scrapbook.

Says who?

Don't do it if it doesn't work for you!

Divide the items in your *School* cubby into items that require action and those that don't. Act on the ones that need it, and for the ones that don't, decide whether they go in the trash, a file folder, or the memento box, and handle accordingly. Anything school-related that has a date attached should be entered on your calendar. Any schedules or upcoming events should go on one of your bulletin boards that are labeled "Commitments," "Possibilities," and "Miscellaneous."

The types of items in your *Work* cubby can vary widely, and only you know how to process them or why they're even there. Whatever actions are required, if you are going to handle a business matter from home, be sure you don't integrate any work papers into your household Stations. Instead, when you are finished acting on them, either put them in your briefcase to take back to the office or carry them to a separate place in your home where you have set up business-related files.

I strongly suggest that if you have a home-based business with no outside office, you make a policy of never using your household desk to handle any business matters, and you never use your business desk to handle any household matters. Keep these two worlds separate, at least as far as the paperwork is concerned, and they will both function more efficiently.

Curb It at the Curb

As you work to handle the paper challenges in your house, remember you can stop a lot of it *before* it starts:

- Stop responding to sweepstakes and surveys. They only get your name on more mailing lists.
- Go to www.dmaconsumers.org and register there with the Direct Marketing Association. You can put your name and address on their do-not-mail list for five years, significantly cutting the flow of junk mail to your home.
- Call 1-888-50PT OUT to have your name removed from credit card solicitation lists.
- To stop a mail-order catalog from coming in the mail, tear your address label off the catalog, write on it "Please remove from mailing list," and mail it back to the company. You can also remove yourself from these lists via phone, though it's usually quicker to handle it through the mail.
- If you donate to a charity in someone's memory (in lieu of sending flowers to a funeral), enclose a note with your donation that says, "This is a one-time donation only. Please do not put me on your mailing list."
- Contact the customer service department of any book club you belong to and tell them you want to change your status in the club so that the monthly selection is not automatically mailed to you. You'll still get the same number of book catalogs from them, but this will eliminate the problem of having to return books you don't want that were shipped because you didn't return the reply postcard in time.

My Most Embarrassing Messy House Story

—Not Finger-Lickin' Good—

BY WILLA F.

I'm not just a bad housekeeper, my car is usually a mess too. About the only time I ever get around to cleaning it is when I know I'll have extra passengers.

One day, I thought I'd done a pretty good job of taking out all the trash and vacuuming the interior since I was driving for the "take kids to school" carpool. But one of my passengers was poking around in a seatback pocket when she came up with a chicken bone—obviously a leftover fast-food drumstick that had been there for who-knows-how-long.

"There's a chicken bone in your car!" she screeched. I tried to make light of it, but she wasn't buying it. Three years later I'm still embarrassed that an old chicken bone was found in my car.

Part 4

From Me to You

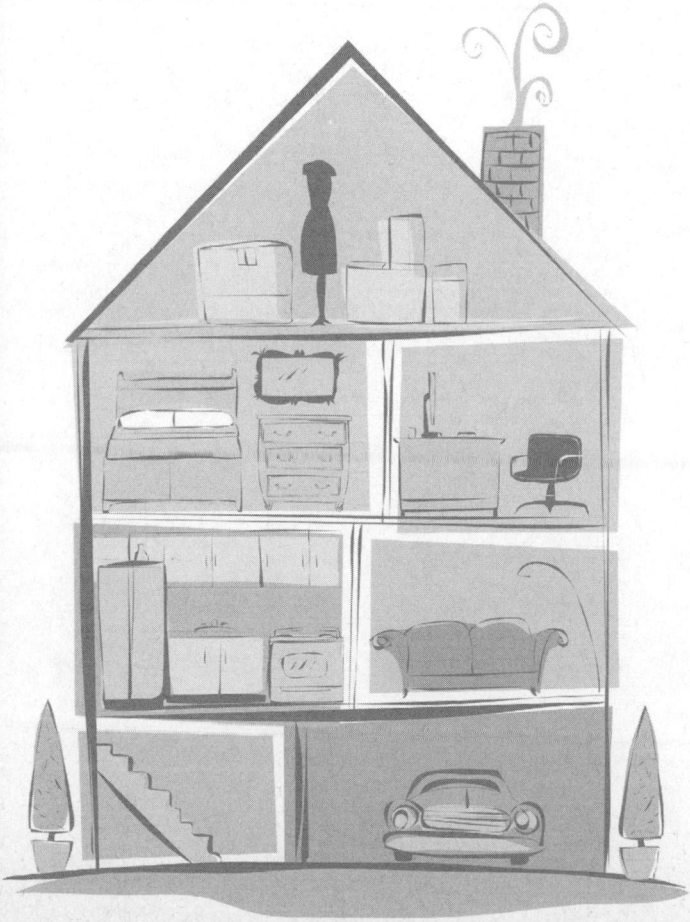

22

My Journey to Clean

For God did not give us a spirit of timidity,
but a spirit of power, of love and of self-discipline.

2 Timothy 1:7

Whether you've gone through my plan for creating a House That Cleans Itself or skipped to this chapter to check out my *own* journey from "messed" to "blessed," I assure you that this plan does work...and will continue to work...for you. I've heard testimonials from many people who have successfully adopted the House That Cleans Itself way of thinking and been thrilled to see how well it works for them. I also know from personal experience...

To be honest, I've struggled with cleaning my entire life.

As a child I was nearly engulfed with the clutter of my toys and belongings, and all I could do was hope my situation would get better as I matured.

As a teenager, the possessions changed but the disaster persisted. Still, I felt sure that once I was on my own I would figure out the whole "cleaning thing."

Once I was on my own and living in an apartment, my cleaning went from bad to worse. I thought maybe I'd get a better handle on it after I was married.

After I was married, it only got harder, especially after one child and then another was added to the mix.

What was I doing wrong?

By the time I was married and had kids, life was a never-ending pile of laundry, an infinite trail of toys that needed to be put away, and a bottomless sink of dirty dishes. *I chose this path,* I would tell myself, even as I hated everything about it...about the cleaning, that is. I loved being a wife, loved being a mom, loved that I was able to work part-time from home, care for the kids, and even attempt to pursue my dream of being a novelist in my "spare time." If not for the cleaning, my life would have been nearly perfect.

Life got even better—though infinitely more complicated—the day my big dream came true and I sold my first mystery novel, *A Penny for Your Thoughts*. In fact, the publisher bought an entire series based on that first book, which meant I would be writing full-time from then on. After a lifetime of waiting for my big break, it had finally come! My family's world changed practically overnight. I quit my part-time job, set up the spare bedroom as an office, and got down to work.

Knowing that I had my hands more than full with this new career, my husband and I soon had to make room in our budget for a housekeeper to come in once a week and handle the deep cleaning. *A housekeeper!* I was ecstatic. Truly, I thought my whole life would change after that.

The one we found was a hard worker, not to mention a lovely lady, and from the very beginning she seemed to do in three hours what usually took me three days to accomplish. (Maybe that should have been a big clue that I wasn't exactly competent in this area.) After her first visit, the place looked great! I knew we would finally have the neat, clean home I had always dreamed of. Mary Poppins had arrived after all.

But within hours of that visit, despite the fact that the house actually sparkled, the mess and clutter began to reappear. After two days, though the rooms were still relatively clean, they looked like a tornado had swept through. By the time the housekeeper returned the following week, the house was so messy it was as if she had never been here. Week after week the same thing happened. I was dumbfounded that so much could go wrong so quickly.

Frustrated, I couldn't even pinpoint the source of the problem. My husband was doing his share of dishes and laundry, but they still piled up. I would complain that the kids were inconsistent with their chores and didn't do enough to help out, yet it was obvious that I wasn't doing enough either, despite the fact that I felt like I was cleaning all day long whenever I had a spare moment. I just couldn't seem to get my act together. When our housekeeper had to pare down her scheduled visits to once every other week our home went from bad to worse.

In desperation I tried creating schedules, plans, chore divisions—all to no avail. Desperate, I prayed to God for help. Fortunately, he answered those prayers, but in a very unique way.

Answered Prayers

For someone who doesn't like housekeeping, I've always had a strange fascination with household hints, such as how to get a blueberry stain from a white linen tablecloth or how to bake fish without stinking up the entire house. (Not that I would ever get around to following these tips, you understand, just that I enjoyed reading about how they could be done if I should ever choose to do them.)

Several years ago I was reading a household hints column in a Sunday paper when I ran across a tip that intrigued me. It said that if you have batteries that are losing their power, you can often get a little extra "juice" out of them by rubbing the ends of the batteries with an emery board. All at once that simple tip conjured up in my brain an idea for a novel. I envisioned a plucky, resourceful young heroine who knows all about household hints. She's hot on the trail of a criminal when the batteries in her flashlight begin to give out. Undaunted, she pulls out the batteries, rubs them with an emery board, puts them back in, and keeps going.

To a fiction writer like me, little tidbits like that are the acorns from which mighty oaks grow. The more I played with the idea of a household-hints expert solving crime, the more I liked it. With my first mystery series drawing to a close, I came up with an idea for a new series about Jo Tulip, a 20-something single gal who writes a "Tips from Tulip" newspaper column. Extremely clever and resourceful, Jo uses her knowledge of household hints not just to write the column but also to pursue and solve mysteries. I pitched the series to my publisher, describing the heroine as "a sort of twenty-first-century female MacGuyver."

My publisher loved the idea and signed me up. But it wasn't until I sat down to begin writing the first book, *The Trouble with Tulip,* that I realized I was a bit out of my element. How was I, this disaster of a housekeeper, supposed to write a series of novels about a household-hints expert?

Well, let's just say they don't call it "fiction" for nothing! Just because I was bad at housekeeping myself didn't mean I couldn't get into the mind of someone who was good at it. I regularly wrote about heroes and villains, private investigators and criminals, government agents and murderers. I figured if I could get into the heads of an FBI agent and a sniper—two things I've certainly never been—then surely I could get into the head of a household-hints expert.

And so I did.

Little did I know that the good Lord had something bigger in mind for me than simply creating a credible character. He also had some giant personal realizations in store. Somewhere along the way, as I spent the next year doing research for the first book in the three-book series about Jo Tulip and her neat and orderly little world, my eyes began to open. The more research I did for Jo, the more it slowly dawned on me what was wrong with my own housekeeping.

I realized I had two major strikes against me.

First of all, I wasn't naturally gifted at housekeeping. In a way, you could say that I was opposite of that—I was actually housekeeping *impaired.* Nothing about maintaining order in my home came naturally to me. Nothing was done by instinct. Like a tone-deaf singer in a choir, I was incapable of doing what needed to be done. I didn't have the talents required.

I had never thought about the fact that housekeeping could require talent and instinct, and not simply knowledge and hard work. But once I admitted that a big part of my problem was rooted not in my behavior but in my brain, I was able to let go of the sorrow and remorse that had plagued me for years. I began to look at my problem more objectively.

Second, I realized that not only did I have no natural housekeeping talents, I also had never been properly taught how to run and maintain a home. My mother is a lovely woman and one of my favorite people on the planet. She's nurturing and sweet and very smart. Her priorities in life have always been as they should be, with God and family at the top of the list. But she is the first person to admit that she's a living example of the "rebound effect" of her own cleanliness-obsessed mother. Refusing to follow in the same footsteps, my mom ranked housekeeping as a far lower priority than her mother had. In our household, the priorities were much more fun things, such as creativity and learning. Along the way, my mother did teach me some basic housekeeping skills, but she rarely modeled them on a day to day basis. Consequently, my yearnings for cleanliness and structure seemed so unreachable, so impossible, that the only way I could even fathom getting my wish for a neat house was to have a visit from Mary Poppins.

How else could we ever get the place clean?

Looking back, I can see that my mother strove mightily to control our clutter. But she too was housekeeping impaired. She too was never taught how it was done. (Her mother was too busy cleaning to teach her daughter how to clean.) And so the cycle continued. As my two kids were reaching their teen years, it struck me that if I didn't do something very drastic, very soon I would be perpetuating the problem of poor housekeeping to the next generation. Their messy bedrooms were living proof of that.

Armed with my new revelations, I decided to make some significant changes. Once I understood that the origins of my housekeeping problems were not character flaws but simply a lack of talent and a lack of knowledge, I became determined to find a way to change my situation. I was already writing the novels about Jo Tulip, housekeeper extraordinaire, but now I made myself a student of her techniques. I wanted to learn, finally, those elusive secrets of real housekeepers.

No, I wasn't concerned with how to get a crayon stain out of a carpet. I was concerned with how to get the junk picked up so you could *see* the carpet! In many cases, housekeeping books didn't speak to me at all. Written by organized and efficient people, they talked about elaborate vertical filing systems for incoming mail and a place for everything and everything in its place. Meanwhile I couldn't even walk from the bed to the bathroom in the dark without tripping on a pile of clothes or slipping on a wayward toy.

Slowly I came to understand the bottom-line truth that had eluded me my entire life: If you're not naturally gifted at housekeeping, and if you've not been given solid housekeeping knowledge, you are your own worst enemy. All the sound, logical, well-meaning advice in the world is not going to help you keep your home clean for very long, especially when that advice is from people who can't relate to either limitation.

What seemed the most demoralizing to me was that my home was set up in such a way that even when it was clean, it felt like a disaster waiting to happen. If I managed to clean the entire house, I didn't find joy in that because with every room I walked through I envisioned how it was going to fall apart soon. Even as I was cleaning, I did it with a heavy heart and the anticipation of the inevitable mess to come.

With these thoughts in mind, through prayer and wise counsel, I was able to make the next logical step in thinking: *What if I rethought the setup and organization of my entire house to fit our family, our lifestyle, our behaviors? What if I fixed not just the problems, but the potential for problems? What if I learned not just how to clean, but how to make my home easier to keep clean?*

Eventually, I theorized, *I could set up my household in such a logical, efficient way that it would practically clean itself.*

The house that cleans itself? Was it possible?

You're holding the answer to that question in your hands! Because

I didn't have a book to guide my way, converting our house took a while—more than a year, if you want to know the truth. But over that time I learned how to work *with* my flaws and weaknesses to overcome the barriers that my family and I had created in our own home. I learned how to make our house fit our behaviors rather than that hopeless battle of doing it the other way around.

My childhood dream of day-to-day organization and cleanliness was realized without a magical nanny in sight!

Now, I don't claim to be a great housekeeper. As I have said, I don't have the natural talent for it, nor do I enjoy it. I struggle to do consciously what most people do innately in the area of home care. But despite my personal impairments, my house is neat and clean most of the time. I no longer yearn to create order from chaos because the chaos is gone.

A House That Cleans Itself?

You bet. We're living in one.

My prayer is that with the help of this book, you can too.

23

A Final Word

Yesterday I got a phone call from a very dear friend whom I've known for 15 years but rarely see in person. Though she used to hang out at my house frequently, we now live several hours apart, and the demands of our lives and families make it difficult to pull off many visits these days. Still, we stay in touch via email and phone as often as we can. During yesterday's phone call, made from her cell phone as she was in her car, she asked me how my writing was going and what I was working on.

"Just putting the finishing touches on my next book," I replied, going on to explain that it was called *The House That Cleans Itself,* and that it was a nonfiction guide to housekeeping.

My statement was met with a long silence.

"Are you still there?" I asked.

"I'm still here!" she squealed. Only then did I realize she was laughing, the kind of laughter so deep and strong that at first it barely makes a sound. The laughing continued, however, and grew louder. It got so loud and went on so long that I kindly suggested she pull to the side of the road lest she have a car accident.

"I'm so sorry," she said finally, and I could just picture her wiping her eyes and trying to pull herself together. "There are many topics I'm sure you could write about, Mindy, but housekeeping *isn't* one of them!"

That set her off into a new bout of laughter. I tried to explain that things around our place aren't like they used to be back when she hung out here, but I'm not sure she believed me. It'll probably take a long visit for her to see for herself.

I've been thinking about that call all day. Believe it or not, her laughter didn't hurt my feelings because if you told me 15 years ago that one day I would write a book on this subject, I would have laughed just as hard. If I am legend in the housekeeping field at all, it's for the messes I have created, not the ways in which I have learned to preempt messes.

But here's the good news. No matter what has come before, *I am a new creature in Christ*. Through his strength and wisdom, I have been transformed. My home has been transformed too.

Things around my house really aren't like they used to be. Not at all. Now that you have read this book, that is my prayer for you as well. After all the hard work of turning your home into a House That Cleans Itself, you'll see lasting and effective change. The system works. Let it work for you.

Take all that extra time and effort you used to devote to ineffective cleaning and give it to God. He's got some wonderful, much better uses for your time and resources than shuffling around a bunch of papers, possessions, dirt, dust, and junk.

God loves you so much.

He's got big plans for your life.

And he's ready to bless you in ways you've never dreamed of.

> *For we brought nothing into the world, and we can take nothing out of it. But if we have food and clothing, we will be content with that* (1 Timothy 6:7-8).

Contact Mindy

If you've got an embarrassing messy house story of your own to share, be sure to send it to me! I reserve the right to share your tale on my website and in future books unless you ask me not to. I promise to keep your name anonymous. Feel free to send your story via regular mail or email.

Address
Mindy Starns Clark
PO Box 38
Dresher, PA 19025

Email
MindyStarnsClark@aol.com

Website
www.mindystarnsclark.com

Be sure to visit my website where you can read about some amazing housekeeping inventions and find more HTCI tips for your home. You can also check out the other books I've written and read chapter excerpts from each.

I look forward to hearing from you!

The Smart Chick Mysteries

Mindy Starns Clark

The Trouble with Tulip

Josephine Tulip is definitely a smart chick, a twenty-first-century female MacGyver who writes a helpful-hints column and solves mysteries in her spare time. Her best friend, Danny, is a talented photographer who longs to succeed in his career...perhaps a cover photo on *National Geographic?*

When Jo's neighbor is accused of murder, Jo realizes the police have the wrong suspect. As she and Danny analyze clues, follow up on leads, and fall in and out of trouble, she recovers from a broken heart, and he discovers that he has feelings for her. Will Danny have the courage to reveal them, or will he continue to hide them behind a facade of friendship?

Blind Dates Can Be Murder

Blind dates give everyone the shivers...with or without a murder attached to them. Jo Tulip is a sassy single woman full of household hints and handy advice for every situation. Her first romantic outing in months is a blind date—okay, the Hall of Fame of Awful Blind Dates—but things go from bad to worse when the date drops dead and Jo finds herself smack in the middle of a murder investigation.

With the help of her best friend, Danny, and faith in God, Jo attempts to solve one exciting mystery while facing another: Why is love always so complicated?

Elementary, My Dear Watkins

When someone tries to push Jo Tulip in front of a New York train, her ex-fiance, Bradford, suffers an injury while saving her—and the unintentional sleuth is thrown onto the tracks of a very personal mystery.

Jo's boyfriend, Danny Watkins, is away in Paris, so she begins a solo investigation of her near-murder. What secret was Bradford about to share before he took the fall? And when Jo uncovers clues tied to Europe, can she and Danny work together in time to save her life?

The Million Dollar Mysteries

Mindy Starns Clark

Attorney Callie Webber investigates nonprofit organizations for the J.O.S.H.U.A. Foundation, giving the best of them grants ranging up to a million dollars. In each book, Callie comes across a mystery she must solve using her skills as a former private investigator. A young widow, Callie finds strength in her faith in God and joy in her relationship with her employer, Tom.

A Penny for Your Thoughts

Just like that, Callie finds herself looking into the sudden death of an old family friend of her employer. But it seems the family has some secrets they would rather not have uncovered. Almost immediately Callie realizes she has put herself in serious danger. Her only hope is that God will use her investigative skills to discover the identity of the killer before she becomes the next victim.

Don't Take Any Wooden Nickels

Just like that, Callie finds herself helping a young woman coming out of drug rehab and into the workforce...who's suddenly charged with murder. What appears to be routine, though, explodes into international intrigue and deadly deception. A series of heart-pounding events lands her disastrously in the hands of the killer, where Callie finds she has less than a moment for a whispered prayer. Will help arrive in time to save her?

A Dime a Dozen

Just like that, Callie finds herself involved in the life of a young wife and mother whose husband has disappeared. But in the search for him, a body is discovered, which puts Callie's job on hold and her new romance with her mysterious boss in peril. Trusting in God, she forges steadily ahead through a mire of clues that lead her deeper and deeper into danger.

A Quarter for a Kiss

Just like that, Callie finds herself on her way to the beautiful Virgin Islands. Her friend and mentor, Eli Gold, has been shot. This unusual—and very dangerous—assignment sends Callie and her boss, Tom, on an adventure together to solve the mystery surrounding the shooting. Though Callie's faith in God is sure, will her faith in Tom survive their visit to the island of St. John?

The Buck Stops Here

Just like that, Callie finds herself in the middle of an intense investigation of a millionaire philanthropist and NSA agent—Tom Bennett, her boss and the man she hopes to marry. Callie overhears a conversation in which her boss implicates himself in her late husband's fatal accident, but Tom's association with the NSA prevents him from answering her questions. Callie must have answers. With God's help she embarks on an investigation that leads to a conclusion beyond her wildest dreams.